Rescue
our world

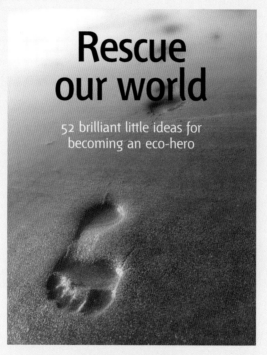

Rescue our world

52 brilliant little ideas for
becoming an eco-hero

Natalia Marshall

brilliantideas

CAREFUL NOW

Saving the world is not something you can do in a day so don't lose interest just because you don't get immediate, dramatic results. Changing small things and working with others will get us there in the end.

The web is constantly being updated so although all web addresses were correct at time of going to press we can't guarantee the availability or content of any site mentioned.

Copyright © The Infinite Ideas Company Limited, 2008

The right of Natalia Marshall to be identified as the author of this book has been asserted in accordance with the Copyright, Designs and Patents Act 1988.

First published in 2008 by
The Infinite Ideas Company Limited
36 St Giles
Oxford
OX1 3LD
United Kingdom
www.infideas.com

A CIP catalogue record for this book is available from the British Library

ISBN 978-1-905940-42-4

Brand and product names are trademarks or registered trademarks of their respective owners.

Designed and typeset by Baseline Arts Ltd, Oxford
Printed in China

Brilliant ideas

Introduction

Take a look at your watch: within the next
hour you could be doing your bit to conserve
the planet's precious resources, reduce
pollution and slow down climate change.
The news these days is full of stories about issues such as soaring
carbon dioxide emissions, global warming, water shortages, toxins
and pollution, most of them man-made. Few people now deny that
our lifestyles are to blame, and that things have to change – sooner
rather than later.

But it can seem very overwhelming. Where do I start? What can I do?
Am I doing enough? These are probably some of the questions you've
been asking.

The good news is that each and every one of us can take steps to
make a difference, and ultimately make the world a better and
healthier place. It may sometimes be tempting to blame far-away
countries and politicians, but the fact of the matter is that we must
all take some kind of responsibility.

And it is very easy to start making a difference; I've done it, and so
can you. Even basic measures such as switching to energy-saving light
bulbs or starting a compost bin are a step in the right direction. I

found using the mantra 'reduce, reuse and recycle' an invaluable building block. Stick to that, and you can't go far wrong!

Once you've got your head around the basics, you'll be surprised how easy it is to go on to the next stage – and the next. Before you know it, you'll find yourself slyly patting your own back, secure in the knowledge you are well on your way to a greener, cleaner existence. If you take on just a fraction of the ideas suggested in this book, you'll be playing your part in a more sustainable future for all of us.

It can be uniquely satisfying to lead a simpler, less resource-hungry life, too. Research shows overwhelmingly that being part of a community (in this case, the eco-gang), appreciating the simple and natural, and acting positively all greatly contribute towards personal happiness. And, what's more, many of the ideas in this book can help you save money.

So, it's a win–win situation!

You certainly don't have to be living in an idyllic rural backwater to 'go green' either. If, like me, you are an ordinary city dweller with a pretty hectic schedule, you can easily adapt your lifestyle so it is less wasteful and more thoughtful. One thing I have learned is that it takes no more time to live green than any other way. And if your home is in a town, you'll have handy access to all kinds of resources to help you on your way.

If you embrace just one idea in this book, that's a brilliant start. Take up a few more, and you're well on your way.

Start with the small things that fit into your daily routine easily and work up to biggies when you feel comfortable. Bear in mind that doing something is better than doing nothing. Our own small actions as individuals add up to a huge global effort, and this is the only way that the planet can recover.

1. Saint or sinner?

Take a long, hard look at your current lifestyle. Is the way you live trashing the planet or nurturing it?

If, like me, you are full of good intentions but decidedly lacking in willpower, it helps to know your weak spots. Let's face it, as a generation we're spoilt rotten, and may not even be fully aware of the detrimental affect our self-indulgent habits are having a on poor old Earth. There's nothing like a bit of self-assessment to kick start the conscience.

If you drive to work in your stonking SUV, do lunch at a fast-food joint, whack up the heating to the max as soon as it gets slightly chilly, do all your shopping at the out-of-town supermarket and throw all the packaging straight in the bin, then you're something of an eco-disaster. Time to change your wasteful and spendthrift habits for a greener, cleaner lifestyle.

Here's an idea for you

Spend a day with a notepad to hand and jot down all the mundane activities you do. Then divide them into two groups: 'wasteful' or 'not wasteful'. If you find it tricky, don't worry – the simple action of writing things down will get you thinking about the way you live.

On the other hand, if you walk or cycle everywhere, lunch on your home-grown salads, eschew chemical cleaning products in favour of lemon juice and bicarbonate of soda, spend your holidays doing voluntary work at your local conservation project and recycle all of your waste, then congratulations, you are fully committed to the environment and well on your way to becoming a green paragon.

Most people fall in between these two extremes. You're definitely aware of what it takes to be green although there are one or two luxuries you're not prepared to give up just yet. The will to change is there, but you've got some way to go before you win the Zayed Prize for the Environment. Make a start by spending a little more time thinking about the impact your actions have on the planet.

2. Hey, big spender

You may baulk at the idea of giving up some luxuries, but going greener can actually boost your happiness levels.

Do you ever feel overwhelmed by excessive choice? It's a 21st century thing, and it can seriously damage your happiness. Call it the satisfaction treadmill: the more options we have, the more we think that there is a perfect choice out there. (Mobile phones are a good example of this.) We're all hyped into seeking perfection, and yet that perfect choice eludes us, so it's back to square one.

How many electric gadgets have you bought to supposedly make life run more smoothly? Do you really need them all? After all, they consume precious resources. What's wrong with a bit of elbow power anyway? Living more sustainably means letting go of some creature comforts. It's about

Here's an idea for you

Jot down half a dozen happy times you can remember. Then, see how many of them tie in with these categories: 1) finding a meaning in life, 2) setting/achieving active goals, 3) belonging to a community, 4) spending time in the natural environment, 5) getting involved with social issues, and 6) helping others. All of these fit in beautifully with more sustainable living, so look forward to your new, green lifestyle.

Defining idea

'Excess choice leads to unfreedom.'
DR BARRY SCHWARTZ, psychology professor

being a bit more thoughtful, and perhaps accepting that we can't all have everything all of the time.

People think that buying more and more 'stuff' will make them happy but research carried out in the US and Europe has shown that our contentment levels haven't really increased since the 1950s despite all our new-found wealth and material choices. It seems the old adage is true: money can't buy you happiness. The gladness gurus have found there's a global minimum living standard that equalises everyone, and after that it doesn't much matter whether you're a billionaire or a binman.

It follows, then, that ditching some of your consumer goodies won't make you any less happy; in fact the opposite could be true. Leading a greener lifestyle certainly involves material sacrifices, but there are tons of compensations. In time, leading a less frantic, less cluttered existence should bring immense satisfaction to you and others around you.

Defining idea

'If you want to live a happy life, tie it to a goal – not to people or things.'
ALBERT EINSTEIN

3. Begin at home

We all have a 'carbon footprint' and the fastest way to reduce yours is to make your home a greener place.

It might be hard to accept but your home is probably your main source of pollution. Everyone's heard the saying 'think global, act local'. Well, your own home is about as local as it gets. And the way you live at home can have worldwide implications for climate change.

Your carbon footprint is the imprint your activities leave on the environment in terms of the amount of greenhouse gases produced, measured in units of carbon dioxide (man-made CO_2 being one of the largest contributors to global warming). Everything you do at home – from the way you dispose of waste to the temperature setting on your thermostat – has an impact on the size of your carbon footprint.

Here's an idea for you

It's quite an undertaking to make your home eco-friendly. If it seems a bit daunting, carry out a mini audit one room at a time. Start with the smallest room in the house – the toilet! Every detail counts: is the loo roll recycled paper, are the light bulbs energy-savers, are the cleaning materials toxic, how much water is flushed, is the tap water overheated? From there, you can progress to the rest of the house.

Defining idea

'A lot of people doing a little bit really is effective.'
DR CHRIS WEST, climate expert

We can all help contain global warming, starting with minimising our footprints. There are simple things you can do today: sign up to a green energy supplier; turn down the central and water heating slightly; only use dishwashers and washing machines at full capacity; don't leave appliances on standby; fit energy-saving light bulbs; insulate your hot water pipes, your loft and your walls; recycle and reuse; save water by harvesting rainwater, reusing 'grey' water (e.g. from your shower) and cutting down on hosing. Best of all, in the long term, doing so will save you cash.

Once you've got the ball rolling, make sure your whole household is involved. Get teenagers to switch off gadgets and lights when not in use; explain to the kids how recycling works and ask them to help you sort your waste into the right bins. Encourage the whole family to cut back on water usage – for instance by not leaving taps running – and get everyone used to having the house slightly cooler. And then just watch your carbon footprint shrink!

4. One more time

Recycling is easier than ever, and almost the entire contents of your waste bin can have a second life.

Even the smallest change in the way we approach the disposal of our waste would make a big difference if universally adopted. Recycling helps in many ways: we send less rubbish to landfill or incineration, and we save valuable materials and energy. For example, recycling aluminium cans saves 95% of the energy used in making a new can. We would all benefit from following the three Rs: *reducing* the amount of rubbish we create, *reusing* stuff we normally throw out, and *recycling* more. All you need to do is become eco-savvy.

To reduce the amount of waste, make sure you buy only the quantities you need and choose products with the least packaging. Store food in resealable containers instead of using cling film or kitchen foil. Use rechargeable batteries (although pricier, they will reduce waste and save you money in

Here's an idea for you

If you're not quite wedded to the idea of recycling yet, try it for one week. In just seven days you will be astonished (and possibly horrified) to see a small mountain of recyclable newspapers, food packaging, bottles, vegetable peelings and lawn cuttings build up. Recycle and your usual bin-bags will shrink to almost nothing!

the long run). Register with the Mailing Preference Service to stop getting junk mail.

You can also cut down on your volume of rubbish by using reusable items: sponges rather than wipes, tea towels rather than kitchen roll. And think of reusing stuff that's old or worn-out: old clothing, towels or bed linen can be used as household cleaning cloths; furniture can be spruced up rather than thrown out (or given to second-hand dealers). Carrier bags can be reused.

Find out about your local facilities and get going. Recyclable items include: aerosols, batteries, cans, paper and cardboard, plastic carrier bags/bottles, CDs, ink cartridges, computers, some furniture, metal, glass, electrical goods, clothes and shoes. Keep separate bins in your house so that you can separate recyclable waste as soon as it's ready. Another great thing about recycling is that you may even become a more efficient householder along the way.

5. Detox your home

'Sick building syndrome' can afflict where you live just as much as where you work. Make your home healthier.

Do you live in a closed box? Our hermetically sealed homes may reduce energy wastage but they can also cause a build up of toxins. It's a sad fact that most of us spend around 90% of our time indoors and windows tend to stay closed except for during the hottest weather. So, you may be living in a toxic time bomb.

Some of the worst culprits for sick building syndrome are chemicals called volatile organic compounds (VOCs), which are gases given off by many household items. They are everywhere: furnishings, cleaning products, polishes, paints, plastics and air fresheners. You can't see VOCs but you can sniff them – the plasticy smell of new carpet is one example – and they can irritate skin, eyes, nose and throat, and cause dizziness, nausea and headaches. Just as importantly,

Here's an idea for you

The easiest and cheapest way to start detoxing your home is simply to open windows more. You don't need to freeze in gale-force winds, but ten minutes a day will let toxins out and fresh air in. It cuts down on the need for air fresheners, too.

Defining idea

'We do not inherit the earth from our ancestors; we borrow it from our children.'
Navajo Proverb

whatever goes down the drain or into the atmosphere eventually ends up in the ocean or back on the ground as rain.

The best way to fight back is obviously to cut chemicals in the home. Choose cleaners, cosmetics and household products that are based on relatively harmless fruit acids and salts, and are biodegradable. Where possible, choose natural materials such as wool carpets, felt underlays, hemp, cotton, linen, wool or hessian fabrics and natural fibre cushions. Switch to organic food.

It is also important to let more of the outside air in. Air circulation dilutes pollutants and helps to keep mould at bay so ensure there is good airflow through wall vents and ducts. And remember that plants are nature's air cleaners so having them inside can help to keep pollutants down.

The jury is still out on whether some VOCs cause more serious illnesses such as asthma, allergies and cancer, but evidence seems to be building up. Tackling these chemicals is war worth waging.

6. Clean but green

It's easy to get hooked on the latest cleaning products that promise a germ-free life, but do you really need them?

Whenever you squirt and spray your home with commercial cleaners, you're adding to your chemical imprint on the environment. It's estimated that fewer than a quarter of the chemicals used in cleaning products have been subjected to a full safety investigation, while others, officially classed as hazardous, are still found as key ingredients.

The overuse of chemical cleaners has also given rise to the so-called 'hygiene hypothesis' – sanitation means less exposure to microbes, which equals more asthma and allergic diseases. We don't need to lead a sanitised life; we need to be an integrated part of the ecosystem, not eradicate it from our homes. It's time to try the softly, softly approach.

Here's an idea for you

Try this recipe for a harmless household cleaner: mix one teaspoon washing soda, four teaspoons borax and one teaspoon liquid soap or detergent with four cups of hot water in a lidded plastic bottle or old spray container. Shake well to blend and dissolve the minerals. Spray the cleaner onto the surface you're cleaning or apply it with a cloth, wiping it off with a rag as you go. For tougher dirt, leave the mix on for a few minutes before removing. Shake the bottle each time before using.

Defining idea

'Man does not live by soap alone.'
GILBERT K. CHESTERTON

There are alternative – and kinder – cleaning materials you can use. Soda crystals (sodium carbonate), also known as washing soda, used to be the most common household cleaning product. They will clean kitchen floors, work surfaces, the draining board and wall tiles. Bicarbonate of soda (baking soda) is also a good cleaner, and if you mix it with water you'll get an alkaline solution that dissolves dirt and grease. Use it dry to lift stains from carpets.

Borax – a naturally occurring mineral, soluble in water – can deodorise, see off mildew and mould, boost the cleaning power of soap or detergent and remove stains. White wine vinegar has many uses. It's a surface cleaner, stain remover and fights limescale; it cuts through grease, deodorises and acts as mild disinfectant. Use half vinegar, half water solution to clean windows, tiles and mirrors. Tea-tree oil is a strong antiseptic and disinfectant.

7. Goodbye pests

There's no need to zap bugs and beasties with eco-hostile pesticides when gentler, safer alternatives do just as well.

When insects make your skin crawl, it's hard to be kind to them. But it's worth overcoming your dislike when you realise that they have a vital role to play in the natural world. So treat them with respect, and shoo them off rather than exterminate them. Using natural deterrents means you'll be helping to maintain the balance of the ecosystem and reducing your use of toxic pesticides.

Moths are understandably annoying when they snack on your favourite jacket but moths and their caterpillars are an important link in the food chain, providing a meal for many mammals, so deter, don't destroy. Aromatic cedar chips in a cheesecloth square or cedar oil in an absorbent cloth will repel them.

Here's an idea for you

Certain essential oils that smell delightful to us and are completely harmless are highly effective at deterring bugs. Find a good supplier and start building up a small collection that includes pure tea tree, neem, rosemary, lavender, eucalyptus, cedar and rose geranium. They can be burned in a water burner, soaked into cotton wool balls, used neat in drops or applied to the skin.

Similarly, put off ants rather than snuffing them out. Ants dislike cayenne pepper, citrus oil (soaked into cotton wool balls), lemon juice, cloves, cinnamon or coffee grounds, fresh garlic or dry crushed mint leaves. Remember to keep counters free of crumbs and sticky spots, cover the sugar and put the honey jar away. If ants still insist on invading, spray them with soapy water.

Effective mosquito repellents include oil of eucalyptus, one part garlic juice with five parts water in a small spray bottle. Strips of cotton cloth can also be dipped in this mixture and hung in areas, such as patios, as a localised deterrent. Neem oil is a safe, natural vegetable oil that contains sallanin, a compound which also has effective mosquito repelling properties. Instead of fly sprays, try natural deterrents such as lemon, cloves, pine and cedar oils.

Using borax to clean hard surfaces is effective against dust mites and a solution of three per cent tannic acid neutralises the protein in dust mite faecal matter that causes most allergic reactions. For head lice, the best repelling oils are tea tree, neem, rosemary, lavender, eucalyptus, and rose geranium, which can be used neat or added to shampoo.

8. Powered up

**All utility services are not equal – some
are much greener than others. Where does
your power come from?**

If you switch on a light and then feel a pang of guilt about the
associated emissions, now might be the time to switch your electricity
to a 'green' supplier. Green energy can be loosely defined as energy
from renewable or sustainable sources – for instance, wind power,
solar energy, biomass energy and small-scale hydro power.

There is plenty of choice for green
electricity but that doesn't mean
they are all good choices. As a result
of confusing information and
unverifiable claims by suppliers,
consumers may not be making the
positive contribution they had
hoped for. Even Friends of the Earth
has withdrawn its online rating
system for green energy suppliers.

Here's an idea for you

Save yourself a lot of hassle by
accessing a website such as
www.uswitch.com that will help you
switch supplier without having to lift a
finger yourself. You can then opt for a
supplier that prioritises environmental
concerns and offers cleaner energy. The
switching service will arrange the
transfer free of charge, including
severing the link to your existing
company, so you can be getting greener
power within days.

27

Defining idea

'Global warming is … one of the most important issues facing all of humanity.'
LEONARDO DICAPRIO

At the moment, opting for a green tariff tends to mean one of three things: 1) 'green' source electricity, where an energy supplier will guarantee to buy, from a renewable generator, a percentage of electricity to match every unit of electricity used by the customer; 2) 'green' fund tariffs designed to support the building of new renewable sources of electricity, environmental causes or new research and development projects; and 3) carbon offset tariffs, which help reduce or offset the carbon dioxide emissions or carbon footprint of the customer.

An ethical power supplier such as Ebico charges all its customers the same price regardless of how they pay. It uses the income generated by direct debit customers to bring down prices for pre-pay and quarterly consumers. Pre-pay customers will see much lower prices, while direct debit payers will still get competitive prices, plus the knowledge they are helping to improve social justice.

You should also remember that even if you are buying green electricity, it is important not to waste power by being as energy efficient as possible – a kilowatt not used is the cleanest kilowatt of all!

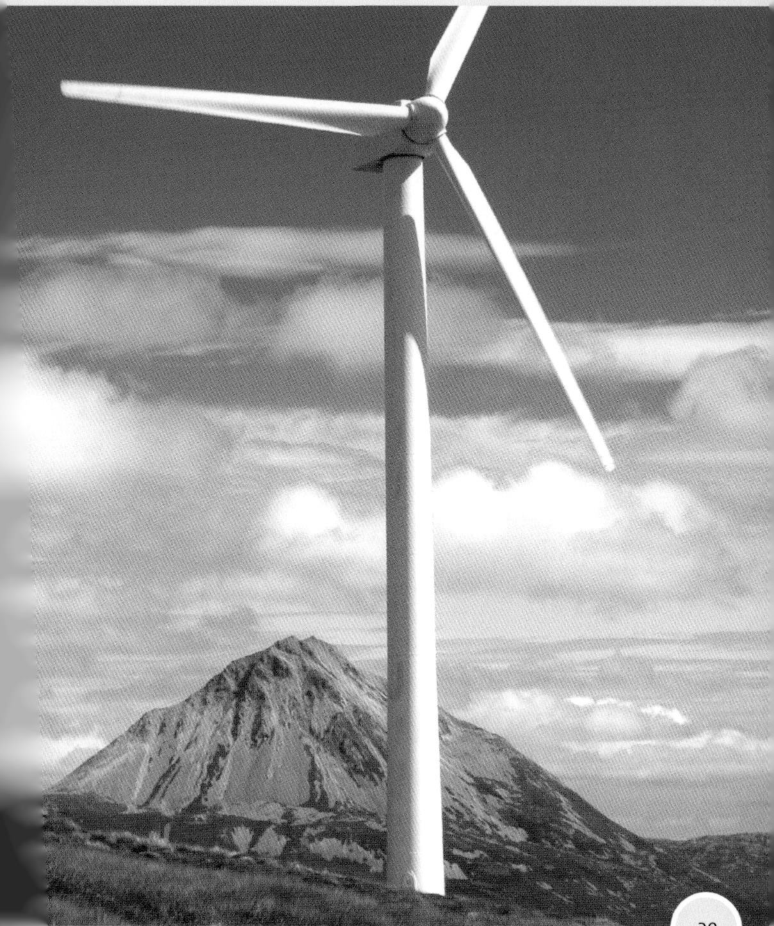

9. Low-impact DIY

We love to add the final decorating touch to our homes, but make sure you choose the least toxic materials.

Of course we all want our houses to look fabulous, but perhaps it's time to start taking more care on the home front: some chemicals and materials that come with the fix-up fetish are major pollutants. Take MDF, or medium density fibreboard, made from wood fibres glued together. It contains formaldehyde, which is an irritant and probable human carcinogen. Cutting and drilling MDF generates fibrous dust that you definitely shouldn't inhale. Ideally replace MDF or particleboard with wheat board, produced from agricultural waste wheat straw and a harmless soy flour binder.

It's not just MDF that releases volatile organic compounds (VOCs) into the air: solvent-based paints, adhesives, flooring, particleboard, and many other building products let off gas, too. That fresh paint

Here's an idea for you

Trust your nose to sniff out the difference between natural paint and hydrocarbon-based paints. One whiff will tell you which one contains strong chemicals. Natural paints don't let off VOCs, are a pleasure to use and can be composted after use to complete the ecological cycle. Ditch the usual petrochemical soup and you'll also reduce your carbon footprint.

Defining idea

'Creativity is the ability to introduce order into the randomness of nature.'
ERIC HOFFER

smell is the calling card of chemicals that can cause headaches, allergic reactions, nausea and tiredness. Many DIY stores now sell paints, varnishes and sealers with minimal or low VOC content so always check the tin before you buy, or better still choose water-based products or less toxic alternatives.

Think about other materials you are using as you fit out your home, and especially avoid those that off-gas, such as plastic or PVC, and whose manufacturing process is highly toxic. Restore rather than replace wherever you can, and use building products made from recycled materials, or reclaimed building materials. You could fit reconstituted doors made of recycled hardboard from lumber mill shavings, which are easy to care for and have good heat insulation.

Only buy as much material as you need for the job, especially paint which doesn't keep well. Don't throw away your white spirit after use as it contaminates the water supply. Let it stand so the sediment can fall to the bottom, then pour off the clean spirit and reuse it. When cleaning water-based paint from brushes and rollers, scrape as much paint as possible onto sheets of newspaper before washing them to minimise the amount of paint flushed down the drain.

10. Read the label

However it comes, it'll have a label to go with it. Get informed on what's inside your day-to-day household products.

Are we living in a toxic timebomb? Nobody really knows, but you can cut back on household chemicals by learning about the worst offenders. It's almost impossible to be 100% green, but the main thing is to be aware, so at least you have the choice. Get into the habit of reading product labels and swapping those that contain toxic stuff for greener alternatives.

Here's a list of the worst culprits to look out for:

- Artificial musks, which are used in many toiletries and cleaning products. Usually described as 'parfum' or 'fragrance' on labels, they are bioaccumulative contaminants in the environment.

- Bisphenol A, a hormone-disrupting chemical found in some polycarbonate plastic, is used for baby feeding bottles,

Here's an idea for you

The garage is often a dumping ground for hazardous materials such as old paints, thinners, adhesives, car oil, methylated spirits and car batteries. Get into the habit of having a regular clear out, and go through each tin or bottle to check exactly what it contains. Ask your local authority for advice on disposing of chemical-based products.

33

refillable water bottles, food containers, CDs and DVDs and electrical appliances.

■ Brominated flame retardants (BFRs) are found in plastics, textiles, furniture and electrical appliances, and are suspected hormone disrupters.

■ Parabens are preservatives found in most cosmetics. They have also been found to mimic oestrogen and have been detected in breast cancer tumours. They are known skin and eye irritants, and have also been linked to sperm damage in males.

■ Phthalates are added to PVC plastics to make them pliable, and to a wide range of cosmetics. They are associated with liver, kidney and testicular damage.

■ Triclosan is a strong antibacterial used in toothpastes, mouthwashes, soaps, deodorants, dish cloths and chopping boards. There are claims that its widespread use is leading to risks to the environment and human health.

11. Green consumers

Ever get the feeling that you're on a consumption treadmill? Jump off now, and join the new breed of consumer.

The eco-movement has spawned a whole new vocabulary, and one of the buzzwords is 'freegan' (free + vegan). Dining on food leftovers from dustbins may have once been the preserve of tramps, but for some it is now more of a lifestyle choice. Greener-than-thou freegans veer away from consumerism and instead scavenge around to meet their needs, including finding food thrown out by shops and restaurants. And why not? Supermarkets simply dump five per cent of their food, most of it completely fit for consumption.

Instead of buying industrially grown, pesticide-sprayed foods shipped half way around the world, some people become wild foragers. They harvest food growing wild in their own communities. An extension of this is to get an allotment. Once you've paid the rental for your patch, everything you grow is yours, meaning you can have a year-round supply of fresh fruit and veg completely free.

Here's an idea for you

Keep an eye out for free-for-all events. There you can exchange goods instead of discarding them, share skills, give presents, eat food, dance, listen to music, sing and generally have fun.

Defining idea

You can cut down on waste by 'precycling' – preventing waste before it happens. Do that by bringing your own packaging, buying in bulk, avoiding junk mail and disposables, extending the life of what you've got and not buying what you don't need. Ardent precyclers carry their own little kit: a washable container, a set of cutlery, a cloth napkin or handkerchief, a bottle of water and a reusable shopping bag.

Then there's 'freecycling' – if you don't want it, pass it on. There are several free goods swapping web-based organisations, notably Freecycle (www.freecycle.org), made up of many local groups across the world. Freecycle groups match people who have things they want to get rid of with people who can use them, keeping usable items out of landfills, reducing consumerism and lessening the impact on the earth.

Skips outside buildings undergoing renovation may just seem full of junk, but to the dedicated low-impact consumer they are a treasure chest for 'skipping' or 'dumpster diving'. You can usually assume that anything in a skip isn't wanted, but if you're not sure ask the property owner before carting it away.

12. Petal power

Houseplants add character to a room, provide a mini carbon-offsetting scheme, and can improve your health.

The psychological and health benefits of houseplants have been unofficially recognised since ancient times, but when an organisation such as NASA starts churning out reports that give this scientific weight, you know that some big issues are at stake. From its research into air pollution inside sealed space habitats, NASA discovered that ordinary houseplants have amazing air purification capabilities.

And what works inside a spacecraft also works in your home. Nature created the human/plant world in balance, so that each supplies the other's needs – we give plants carbon dioxide when we breathe out, and they give us oxygen. Plants decrease carbon dioxide concentrations and air temperatures in buildings as well as raising humidity. If we all filled our homes with houseplants, it would go a

Here's an idea for you

Look after your houseplants to maximise their detox properties. Plants with broad glossy leaves appreciate an occasional wipe over with a damp cloth. Their 'lungs' are in the leaf surface and a layer of dust will stop them breathing.

Defining idea

'I go to nature to be soothed and healed.'
JOHN BURROUGHS

little way towards offsetting some of the CO_2 each house inevitably produces.

NASA also found that foliage plants had an excellent ability to remove VOCs and stop people experiencing those queasy or 'sick building' feelings without being harmed themselves. Spider plants, for example, can remove up to 96% of carbon monoxide, a toxic exhaust gas. These are some of the most effective detoxifiers: dragon tree (dracaena), ivy, ficus (either weeping fig or the sturdy rubber plant), philodendron, spider plant, peace lily, ferns (all varieties), chrysanthemums, gerbera and palms.

Take the same kind of care as you would for outdoor gardening: choose the right plants for your conditions, plant them in healthy soil, give them fertiliser and water properly, and keep an eye on things. Don't overwater or overfeed your plants. Only give them a drink when the top layer of soil is dry. Only feed them (with natural fertilisers) during the active growing season because overfeeding makes them weak and susceptible to disease.

Re-pot your plants about once every other year. Do it in the spring or summer when the plants are actively growing.

13. Warm and cosy

Keep heat in with top-notch insulation and glazing and save money by reducing energy wastage.

You don't have to be a genius to work out that if you cut back on fuel usage you will save yourself a packet, and obviously it has environmental benefits too. There are basically two biggies when it comes to saving energy: 1) use less power and 2) don't let heat escape.

Insulation is the key to any ecologically sound home. Heat loss through walls and roofs can account for as much as 80% of heating costs. In older houses, insulating cavity walls and lofts makes the most difference. Your home could also be losing 20% of its heat through single-glazed and poorly insulated window frames. Double glazing (using Forest Stewardship approved wood, of course) can halve these losses.

Here's an idea for you

It costs next to nothing to eliminate draughts and wasted heat. Fix a brush or seal on your exterior doors, fill gaps in floorboards and skirting and have thick curtains to insulate windows. But don't suffocate! Open fireplaces and gas heaters need some ventilation to stop the build-up of toxic fumes.

Watch how much hot water you waste. Always turn off hot water taps when you're not using them. An ordinary shower uses less than

Defining idea

half of the water needed for a bath. Look at the water temperature setting, too: it doesn't need to be set higher than 60°C. Match the right-sized pan to the amount of food you're cooking, and keep lids on. Only use as much water as you need inside the kettle.

Appliances can be another heat-sink on your bank balance and the environment. Fridges are on 24/7 so they use a huge amount of power. Always close the door quickly to stop cold air from escaping and don't put hot or warm food straight into the fridge. Save energy by turning off your dishwasher before it completes its drying cycle, leaving the heat inside to do the work. Don't leave TVs, stereos and DVD players on standby, or mobile phones or laptops on charge unnecessarily.

Replace old appliances with energy-saving models displaying an appropriate logo or certification. If your boiler is over 15 years old, consider replacing it with a high-efficiency condensing type. They can help you save up to a third on your heating bills.

14. Burn naturally

**If you're hankering after a real fire, you
need to make sure you choose a fuel
that's as clean as possible.**

More and more of us are unblocking old fireplaces or flues and
getting down and dirty in the wood pile. Wood is a versatile fuel and
can be burned in many different forms and in loads of different
appliances. It can heat one room or the whole house, and it can
produce hot water and heat for cooking.

But hold on – if you're keen on an
open fire, you're living with
massive heat loss: as much as 90%
of the heat will go straight up the
chimney. In terms of efficiency, a
closed wood burner is far better,
especially the new breed of clean
burning stoves. Pellet stoves are
another efficient option. They burn
carbon neutral pellets made from sawmill waste and have fans to
distribute the heat around the house.

Here's an idea for you

Store your wood outside, raised off the
ground and covered. Bringing green
wood indoors to dry can cause the
growth of mould spores indoors which
could trigger allergies. Put old ash to
good use in your compost heap. It's
high in potash and a good garden
fertiliser.

Defining idea

*'It is folly to punish your neighbour by
fire when you live next door.'*
ESKIMO PROVERB

Bear in mind that burning anything
will release some emissions: carbon
dioxide and traces of carbon
monoxide, particulates and volatile
organic compounds. Logs are better
than coal in this respect, though, as
they are from a renewable source
in the sense that you are only
releasing the carbon dioxide that
was absorbed as the tree grew.

These are some of the golden rules for a warm, environmentally
sound fire: burn small, hot fires using seasoned wood, ideally with
logs around 10–15 cm (4–6 inches) in diameter; source logs locally
(e.g. from a local tree surgeon, or from dead trees that have fallen);
never burn rubbish, plastics, glossy paper or polystyrene, treated or
painted wood, particulate-board or plywood; and make sure the fire
is getting enough air – check that the air inlet is open wide enough
to keep the fire burning briskly and with minimum smoke.

Softwoods tend to catch easily and burn quickly, and so are good for
kindling but don't have much staying power. Good, harder woods to
burn are ash, beech, hornbeam, hawthorn, crab apple and wild
cherry.

15. Natural energy

**Want to see your energy bills plummet?
Then harness natural energy sources and
go green at the same time.**

Renewable energy, such as solar and wind power, can be used
without depleting natural resources and with minimal pollution.
And, better still, if you produce excess energy you can sell it back to
the national grid. However, do be realistic about its energy output –
in some cases you'll be looking at 20 years plus to recoup your costs.
Also, check out any building restrictions and rules with your local
authority, and get it installed by professionals.

With solar power, there are
basically two kinds: solar water
heating, which simply heats a tank
of water, and solar photovoltaic
(PV), which uses daylight to create
electricity. The easiest for most
householders is a solar water
heating system, which is very low

Here's an idea for you

As a cost-effective way of finding your
way through the alternative energy
maze, bring in a professional
environmental auditor who can assess
your individual potential in energy
saving. You may have to pay them a
fee, but you'll claw that back when your
utility bills fall.

maintenance and can provide about half of your domestic hot water needs over the year. PV systems generate no greenhouse gases and can be used on any building with a strong enough roof. Prices vary depending on size: the more juice you want, the bigger the system you'll need.

To generate plentiful power and recoup your costs, micro wind turbines need to sit in a consistently windy spot, preferably in a remote rural area with no buildings or trees nearby that might interfere with the wind force. There are many planning issues so wind power is not something to be undertaken lightly.

The use of flowing water to generate power is probably the oldest form of renewable energy. Hydropower produces no waste products during operation and once up and running it's free. Small hydro systems can supply electricity directly to the home or can be used to charge batteries or as a back up to a diesel generator.

Ground source heat pumps make use of energy stored in the earth through a series of pumps and pipes. Although pricey to install, they have very low maintenance costs. They work best with heating systems designed to run at a lower water temperatures – for example, underfloor heating.

16. Good wood

Wood is a wonderful asset to any home but be eco-aware by making sure it comes from sustainable sources.

There's nothing like natural wood for beauty, durability and versatility. Wood is warm in winter and helps keep rooms cool in the summer; it lends itself to both modern and contemporary styles; and, conditioned with natural non-toxic waxes or oils such as linseed, it will last you a lifetime.

While we're not yet at the stage of treating wood as a rare commodity, we do need to go easy on this most precious of resources. Approximately half of the Earth's original forest cover has been cut down and, of the half that remains, only around one tenth is protected, and most of this is badly managed. This is where you come in: you can do your bit by increasing demand for certified timber, particularly for tropical

Here's an idea for you

Some of the best quality wooden flooring and other fittings is vintage stuff that is found in reclamation or salvage yards, so get to know your local suppliers. Older wood still in good condition will have stood the test of time – Victorian pine floors, for instance, were originally made from very dense first growth forest timber, far superior to most new wood sold these days.

Defining ideas

'Forests are the lungs of our land.'
FRANKLIN D. ROOSEVELT

*'What we are doing to the forests of
the world is but a mirror reflection of
what we are doing to ourselves and to
one another.'*
MAHONDAS K. GANDHI

hardwoods. If you're buying new
wood, source products that are
Forest Stewardship Council (FSC)
certified.

The FSC is an international
organisation that promotes care of
the world's forests and FSC
certification guarantees your
timber comes from a well-managed
forest. Forests contain as much as 90% of the world's terrestrial
biodiversity. Forests purify the air we breathe, provide life-saving
medicines and are key to controlling soil erosion and preventing
flooding.

Obviously it's even more environmentally sound to simply repair,
restore or adapt a wooden product you already have. You may need
to get a pro in for the job, but it could still be cheaper than buying
something new and it's far better for the world's forests. It's also
worth thinking whether friends, neighbours or community groups
could use the spare timber or off-cuts from your DIY or home
improvement project. Some quality timber items, such as doors,
fireplaces and kitchen units might be worth selling on.

'Buy it with care, treat it fair' should be your mantra when it comes
to all things wooden.

17. If in drought...

Conserving water at home should become part of your day-to-day routine. It couldn't be simpler.

Water is something that many of us take for granted, not thinking twice before lazing back in a deep bath or carelessly leaving the sprinkler on in the garden. Global water consumption has risen almost tenfold in the last century, and UNESCO has predicted that water shortage will be a major global problem by 2020, bringing with it disease, malnourishment, crop failure and environmental damage. So each and every one of us needs to take responsibility for the amount of water we consume.

One of the easiest ways of saving water in the kitchen/laundry is to install water efficient appliances and ensure that you fill them right up each time. If you wash by hand, use minimum detergent to cut back on rinsing, and use a plugged

Here's an idea for you

Toilets use about 30% of the total water consumed in a household. If your loo is not a modern dual-flush, install a cistern displacement device. This is an inflated plastic bag that sits inside the cistern and saves about one litre of water with every flush. It doesn't sound like much, but given that the average household flushes up to 5000 times per year, that's an awful lot of water!

Defining ideas

'The frog does not drink up the pond
in which it lives.'
Chinese proverb

'When the well's dry, we know the
worth of water.'
BENJAMIN FRANKLIN

sink or a bowl of water. Try to capture 'warm-up' water for rinsing dishes, washing fruit and vegetables, or other cleaning jobs. If you have a garbage-disposal unit, don't use it. They use about 30 litres of water per day and send a lot of extra rubbish into the sewers.

In the bathroom, take showers rather than baths, and keep them short. Remember that power showers can use more water than a bath in less than five minutes. Turn the tap off when brushing your teeth or shaving. A running tap uses about five litres of water per minute.

On the outside, install a rainwater tank that collects runoff from roofs and gutters for garden use. You could even ask your local council about getting it connected to the toilet for flushing. When watering the garden, make sure it's just the plants you water – not the paving!

Wash your car sparingly and reuse water from inside when you can. If you don't have to drive too far, visit a commercial car wash that recycles wash water.

18. Shop smart

How do we shop ethically? Sounds like an easy question but the answer is still devilishly convoluted.

Going eco-shopping means knowing more than just what's on your groceries list. On the one hand, we're told that we should eat food that is locally produced and not air freighted hundreds of miles; on the other, we're under pressure to support producers in far-away developing countries. We're expected to know the difference between organic and free-range foods, stay abreast of flashpoints (palm oil, bluefin tuna, PVC), and only buy goods with certain eco-labels attached. Confusing? Of course. Guilt making? You bet.

The rights and wrongs of living green seem to be shifting faster than the sands in the Sahara, so the best starting point is simply to be informed about what you buy. Get to know what's inside the products, whether they're organic or not, how they are produced, and where and how they are delivered.

Here's an idea for you

How mad is it to bottle and ship water round the world and pay up to 10,000 times the price of tap water? Buy bottled water from local sources. Better still, use your taps!

Defining idea

'He who buys what he does not need steals from himself.'
Author unknown

To some extent you have to pick your battles. If your main concern is climate change, then you'll want to know how far your goods have travelled. (Some retailers are now providing point-of-sale freighting information.) If you're worried about chemicals, then you'll go for organic and natural. If you hate the thought of producers getting a raw deal you'll buy Fairtrade. And if you deplore the way that supermarket giants have squeezed supply chains and taken over neighbourhoods then you'll shop at small, local shops instead. In the 21st century, we consumers have a choice – so use it wisely.

Only buy what you *really* need and avoid cut-price offers unless they can be stored indefinitely. Avoid excessive packaging by buying in bulk or choosing loose produce rather than packaged fruit and vegetables. Use your own carrier bags. Opt for eco-friendly stuff with a validation logo or accreditation, such as the not-so-endangered fish recommended by the Marine Stewardship Council (www.msc.org). Seek out electricals that have an on/off switch rather than a standby-only option. Greenpeace has a guide to greener mobile phones and PCs (www.greenpeace.org).

19. Wild things

**Go from shopaholic to cropaholic – scour
your neighbourhood for freebie natural
berries, nuts, leaves and fungi.**

It wasn't that long ago in evolutionary terms that we were hunter-
gatherers, and I like to think that there's still a lingering echo of the
forager in us all. There's a whole host of wonderful seasonal produce
growing wild in the hedgerows, fields, river banks and coasts, and
it's there for us harvest – free of charge and as green as can be.
Spending a day out looking for goodies such as berries, leaves,
seaweed, roots, nuts and fungi is immensely satisfying and it's
something the whole family can enjoy.

If you're new to wild foods, your
best bet is to go out armed with a
good illustrated book, ideally one
with recipes – you'll need to know
how to prepare those four kilos of
fresh nettle leaves. Obviously, you
need to be careful about what you
harvest, especially when it comes to
berries and fungi. If in doubt, don't

Here's an idea for you

Don't feel left out if you live in a city:
you can still get out there and gather
wild foods. Look for churchyards, sports
grounds, municipal gardens, canal
towpaths, disued railways and, in fact,
any open, green space – all can yield
rich pickings for the modern hunter-
gatherer. However, it's best to avoid
sites right next to main roads.

Defining idea

'Nature provides a free lunch, but only if we control our appetites.'
WILLIAM RUCKELSHAUS

touch it. In no time you'll become a bit of a botanist.

Be careful about where you traipse, too. If you're on private property, golf courses, commercial land, sensitive nature reserves or farmland, ask permission from landowners and farmers before rummaging through hedgerows, even though what you're taking is probably unwanted and considered to be a weed. Another general rule is to only pick the leaves, stems and fruits of plants, don't dig or pull them up.

Some popular wild foods include blackberries, damsons and sloes; young dandelion leaves and garlic mustard (great in salads); nettles (the young, tender, vitamin-C rich tops can be used like spinach); and mushrooms of all kinds. Mushrooms are ready to be gathered in the late summer/early autumn but some are poisonous so you must know your fungi before you tuck in.

A more exotic example would be marsh samphire, which is found in the summer months along the coast and looks a bit like cacti. Boiled, it makes a fabulous accompaniment to fish.

20. Green gadgets

It's worth checking out the new breed of 'eco-friendly gadgets' designed to help you save energy and cash.

The problem with consumerism is that it has boosted our appetite for electronics at the same time as we're under pressure to conserve energy. Thankfully, some manufacturers are moving towards smart electronics that only use energy when needed and there are green options for the eco-conscious. Some products are really just eco-toys but others genuinely do help save energy or other resources.

Once a dull-but-worthy technology that simply sat on roofs, solar power has shrunk into a tool we can all make use of. You can now get small solar-powered devices that run virtually all handheld devices including MP3 players and mobile phones. There are solar powered wearables, too, such as baseball caps with integral solar

Here's an idea for you

Work out how much electricity your appliances on standby use up. Switch off everything else except the stuff you leave on standby and watch your electricity meter spin round for an hour. Take a kW unit reading and cost it from your last bill, then multiply it by 24 to see how much you could save in just one day. Scary stuff ...

panel and fan, and backpacks that act as a mobile power source designed to charge your gadgets while on the move.

Another gadget designed to save electricity is a standby cut-off, featuring a switch and two wireless remote control sockets. You plug it into a wall socket and then plug your TV, stereo, set top box, computer etc into the socket. Just flick the switch when you leave the house and you know you're not wasting energy.

Wind-up gadgets, such as the radios invented by Trevor Bayliss, are also enjoying a flush of success, particularly with the debut of the first digital audio broadcasting (DAB) wind-up radio, wind-up torches and wind-up mobile phone chargers.

Light emitting diode (LED) lightbulbs are the environmentally friendly lights of the future. They last for around 30,000 hours (vs. 15,000 for a normal low energy bulb), saving you even more money and energy. They don't get very hot, they don't contain harmful chemicals (low energy bulbs can contain mercury), and tend to be smaller and lighter, so saving on transport and packaging.

21. Clothing care

By all means stay fresh, but launder and iron your clothing with the minimum use of chemicals and energy.

It's surprising me how many people routinely wash their laundry at very high temperatures. What a waste of electricity! It shortens the life of fabric, too. Modern, highly efficient detergents are designed so you can usually reduce the temperature of your wash to around 30°C without compromising on cleanliness. You can get away with a shorter wash, too.

There are many other environmentally friendly steps you can take with clothes care. Always wait until you've got a full load before using your washing machine – using the 'half load' programme does not save you half the energy, water or detergent. Clean your washing machine occasionally by clearing out filters and running it empty on a hot cycle with a little white vinegar in the detergent compartment to clear soap deposits. This will help prolong the life

Here's an idea for you

For hand-wash items, try biodegradable soap flakes. Dissolve them thoroughly first, keep the water no more than tepid and use cold water for rinsing. Splash a little vinegar into the final rinse to remove all the suds.

Defining idea

'The necessity of practising economy
should be evident to every one.'
ISABELLA BEETON

of your washing machine and keep it working efficiently.

Use eco-friendly laundry products whenever possible. If you love the idea of never having to buy detergent again, suspend your scepticism and give laundry balls a go. These little plastic reusable spheres are used in place of soap, meaning you use less water and less electricity as you bypass the rinse cycle. They work by producing ionised oxygen that naturally activates the water molecules. The balls soften the water so no fabric conditioner is needed and also minimise colour fading. Each pack of three should last for 1000 washes.

It's obviously more eco-friendly to dry laundry outside rather than tumble dry it. However, if you must, help it work efficiently by leaving plenty of space for clothes to move around and don't run it for too long – over-drying the clothes makes ironing harder and wastes energy.

Dry cleaning has to be one of the most environmentally unsound ways of laundering clothes. The strong smell of chemicals is the giveaway. The only way around this problem is to reduce the amount of 'dry-clean only' clothing you buy.

22. Step outside

Take a tour round the outside of your home and see just how much harm it could be doing to the planet.

Because we spend around 90% of our time indoors, it's all too easy to focus on the inside of your home when it comes to green issues. But there are certainly steps you can take on the outside to improve its eco-status.

Start by thinking 'reclaimed timber'. Old wood is well seasoned, affordable and doesn't plunder resources. Use it for fencing, gates and decking. Old railway sleepers can be bought cheaply and are great for creating beds or sectioning off parts of the garden. For decking, there are some recycled plastic options that look good and are very easy to maintain. Garden furniture is also now available in this recycled material, and there are even slate-effect roof tiles made from recycled plastic that look the part and won't crack and age like natural slate.

Here's an idea for you

Think about your roof. Does the snow or frost there melt faster than on your neighbour's roof? Well, that's because your loft insulation isn't doing its job. Up to 25% of heat is lost through un-insulated roofs, so make sure you have the recommended 11 inches (270mm) of insulation to keep your house warmer and reduce your annual fuel bill.

Defining idea

'What is the use of a house if you haven't got a tolerable planet to put it on?'
HENRY DAVID THOREAU,
American writer and philosopher

No eco-warrior's garden is complete without a water butt to collect rainwater run-off from the gutters. Similarly, your garden will NOT have a patio heater – they are spawn of the devil in the eyes of environmentalists, kicking out the emissions of a speeding truck. Put on a jacket or go indoors!

If you're a charcoal briquette fan, cancel that barbecue! These briquettes release carbon monoxide, particulates and harmful volatile organic compounds (VOCs) thanks to their chemical additives. Propane, also called liquid petroleum gas (LPG), burns more cleanly than charcoal briquettes, meaning less localised pollution, but it is still a CO_2 baddie. Real grill jockeys insist on natural wood charcoal and, luckily, it's also the most environmentally friendly too. Charcoal is carbon neutral.

There's a growing trend for homes to be brilliantly floodlit all night. This is complete waste of electricity, irritating to neighbours and disruptive to wildlife. If you install security lighting, make it movement sensitive and timed to go off after a short while.

23. Choose organic

Buying and eating organic food is one of the simplest ways to achieve a cleaner, greener lifestyle.

Sure, some people insist that there are no health benefits to organic produce. However, when governments start advising you to top and tail carrots to get rid of the most toxic pesticides (which is what happened in the UK), you know it's time to switch to organic.

As well as helping you ingest fewer chemicals, organic food is also softer on the environment than factory-farmed produce. To be organic, the food must have been produced on an organic farm, which is free of any chemical fertiliser or pesticides. Animals on organic farms must be reared and slaughtered in a humane manner. When you look at a product that claims to be organic, in most cases you will see the symbol of an organic agency (e.g. the Soil Association).

Here's an idea for you

Organic price tags can hurt. If cost is an issue, list the main five or six foods that you eat and test whether you can afford to make them 'organic must-haves'. Go for bulky basics (bread, potatoes, milk, meat, eggs, root vegetables and cereals), which could have a real impact on your diet. It's less important that smaller items, such as garlic, dips or herbs, are organic.

Defining idea

'Nature is a self-made machine, more perfectly automated than any automated machine.'
ERIC HOFFER

The easiest way to try out organics is to join a 'box scheme'. In these, a colourful selection of the freshest possible seasonal produce will be delivered to you from an organic farm, normally weekly. Most schemes offer a range of boxes, each with a set selection of farm produce, but you can often mix and match. You usually also have the option of organic extras such as cheese, honey, preserves, meat and eggs.

Farmers' markets are also becoming increasingly popular, and you can see why. As well as giving you an opportunity to wander around looking at – and tasting – different kinds of foodstuffs, you have the chance to chat with the producers, and learn about their growing or manufacturing methods.

Even the supermarkets have undergone a sea change in the past few years and most of them offer a good range of organic foods. Prices still remain comparatively high, but the stores say they are simply reflecting the extra costs needed to produce organic food and that profit margins are the same as for all their other food.

24. Home-made goodies

Prepare your own preserves, pickles, cordials and dried herbs to maximise seasonal produce and save cash.

Making your own preserves puts you back in touch with the seasons and a food's origins, and is really just another way of enjoying local produce. And of course you are fully in control of what goes in – no artificial additives, preservatives or sweeteners. You can use organic ingredients (alongside Fairtrade sugar, of course), perhaps grown in your own garden or allotment or just plucked from the hedgerows that morning. They make fantastic gifts, too.

A traditional jam is made by cooking whole or cut fruit with sugar, while a jelly is made by cooking the juice of the fruit with sugar. Always use fruit that's in peak condition, preferably slightly underripe, when the pectin (setting agent) content will be at its highest.

Here's an idea for you

Slow drying apples is a good way of making them last. Dried apple can be added to cereals or cakes or eaten on its own as a healthy snack. Try peeling, coring and cutting apples into rings and hanging them on strings somewhere very warm, or drying them in a very low oven.

Defining idea

Defining idea

'In the early autumn, plums of various kinds are to be bottled and preserved, and jams and jellies made.'
MRS BEETON

You can make your own organic, deep-hued wines and cordials from soft fruits such as blackcurrants, sloes, elderberries and raspberries. It you prefer something a little stronger, add fruits to strong spirits – rum, brandy or gin – and allow the colours and flavours to infuse for a few weeks.

In chutneys, vinegar rather than sugar is the main preserving agent, and is cooked with vegetables or orchard fruits, or other fruits such as peaches, bananas, mangoes and apricots. Pickles are normally made with vegetables, which are preserved whole or in large pieces in vinegar flavoured with spices. The veggies are normally pickled raw to preserve their crunchy texture.

Grow your own chillies, garlic and herbs and add them to your favourite oil such as olive or groundnut and allow to infuse for a couple of weeks. Elegantly presented in a nice recycled bottle these make ecologically sound gifts, too. You can grow your own supply of organic herbs in a pot, window box or garden, and dry them before they die off. Store your dried herbs in airtight containers, preferably not plastic, away from sunlight and use them within a year.

25. Natural first aid

Why spend a fortune on synthetic medicines when there are perfectly acceptable natural alternatives available?

It's hard to believe, but dumped over-the-counter medicines form a substantial part of the hazardous waste in landfill sites. While I wouldn't suggest swapping important drugs for herbs or oils, there is surely a place for natural remedies in the medicine cabinet for minor conditions. Many of them can provide considerable relief, most are non-toxic and often suitable for children (although always check on the packet).

Best used in gel form, aloe vera is good for all kinds of minor wounds and burns, including sunburns. The herb calendula in salve form is an anti-inflammatory, astringent and antiseptic and can also be used on burns as well as rashes, cuts and sprains. Camomile is a pleasant smelling herb is used as an anti-

Here's an idea for you

Try out remedies on yourself and your family to see which produce the best results. It's important that you actually enjoy using the product because research shows that the placebo effect works alongside the medicinal one to produce a stronger healing experience.

Defining idea

'If I'd known I was going to live so long, I'd have taken better care of myself.'
LEON ELDRED, AMERICAN HUMORIST

inflammatory as well as a digestive aid. It is good for nappy rash. Another anti-inflammatory is the herb St John's wort, which can be blended with oil to massage aching muscles.

Ginger (capsules, tea bags and crystallised) has antispasmodic and gas-relieving properties to soothe digestive upsets. Ginger also has been shown to relieve motion sickness. Most herbal laxative teas rely on senna, often combined with herbs such as cinnamon, fennel, liquorice and ginger to mask its bitter taste. The sedative properties of valerian tincture make it useful for relieving anxiety, insomnia and tension. A powerful antimicrobial, goldenseal (in capsules or powder) is effective against a variety of micro-organisms that cause traveller's diarrhoea. The powder has antiseptic properties and can be sprinkled onto cuts or wounds to stop bleeding.

Distilled witch hazel has mild astringent, antiseptic and anti-inflammatory properties, so it's handy for insect bites and skin irritations. Lavender oil also offers relief for stings and bites. Tea tree oil has potent anti-fungal and antiseptic properties, making it a useful remedy for athlete's foot, minor wounds, insect repellent and headlice. A potent antibiotic and antiviral, eucalyptus oil is good for treating colds and sinus infections when used as a steam inhalation.

26. Eco-dressing

More and more fashion brands are jumping on the ethical bandwagon, so there's plenty of choice out there.

Many clothes are made from synthetic materials such as nylon and polyester, which come from highly polluting petrochemicals whose manufacture contributes to climate change. They are also non-biodegradable, which means they are difficult to dispose of. Natural fibres aren't all squeaky clean, either. Cotton uses more pesticide per plant than almost any other crop, causing damage to the environment and the people who farm it.

But the fashion industry, or parts of it, is now turning its attention to producing a new breed of environmentally friendly clothing, or eco fashion. Eco fashion is manufactured using low carbon, non toxic processes, and includes organic clothing, recycled textiles and materials such as plastic drinks

Here's an idea for you

To avoid wasteful hoarding, get together with a few friends and have a clothes swap party. If each guest brings along a bag full of wearable but unwanted clothes, chances are you'll each be able to swap a few outfits over a glass of wine or two. Any remaining items can be donated to charity.

Defining idea

'Fashion passes, style remains.'
COCO CHANEL

bottles. Yes, it does come with a higher price tag, but wouldn't you rather pay a little more knowing that workers aren't being exploited and the planet trashed?

You can do your bit by paying attention to the materials you buy. For instance, organic cotton is grown without the use of chemical pesticides and insecticides, and organic cotton garments are often also free from chlorine bleaches and synthetic dyes. Hemp needs few or no agrichemicals to grow, and at the same time it binds and enriches the soil with its deep roots. Linen is made from flax, another traditional fibre crop which needs fewer chemical fertilisers, and less pesticide than cotton. Bamboo has recently been developed as a clothing fibre, which is great for eco-fashion as it's highly sustainable, and produces clothing that is soft, breathable and fast drying.

You can find Fairtrade products by looking out for the logo, which guarantees that that product has been made in line with standards as set out by the Fairtrade Foundation. Once you've bought ethically, dispose of your old clothes with the same care. Take old clothing to charity shops or recycling points, or customise your own clothing to extend its life.

27. Skin deep

Pamper yourself by all means, but could your beauty products be doing you – and the planet – more harm than good?

Like many other industries, the world of beauty is undergoing something of a revolution, with manufacturers racing to get new organic or 'ethical' products onto the shelves as fast as they can. As consumers become more savvy about ingredients and sourcing, some brands have been driven to rethink their whole ethos, right down to their packaging and their involvement with the communities they source from. And it's just as well.

The average Western bathroom cabinet is stuffed with shampoo, mouthwash, toothpaste, creams, shaving gels and hygiene products. These products contain a wide variety of chemical substances, the safety of which remains questionable. There are over 1000 chemicals currently in use that are suspected to have harmful effects.

Here's an idea for you

Watch out for 'greenwash' (bogus or inflated environmental claims). Words like 'natural', 'environmentally sound' or 'safe' often can't be substantiated. Read the small print first, and look out for specific information that backs up claims and certification from recognised bodies.

Defining idea

Some of these survive the journey through sewage works into the sea. Our skin soaks up 60% of what we put on it, and ultimately chemicals can end up travelling throughout our entire systems.

The term 'natural' is now highly dubious – a product has to have only 1% natural ingredients to earn this moniker! That said, there are a number of genuinely natural products on the market. The best ones will provide a list of ingredients, and most of these ingredients will have familiar names. (Natural soaps, for instance, will contain coconut, corn, soy or olive oil.) Look out for the word 'organic' instead, and especially for logos such as the Soil Association's, which will guarantee 95% organic contents.

There are other ways to be ethical. Take a look at the way the manufacturer runs its company. Aside from what it puts into its products, it should have a responsible attitude towards the environment. Ask about company policies on chemical usage, recycling, employment, health and safety. Support companies whose policies you agree with.

Other things you can do include wearing less make-up! And try to avoid synthetic fragrances and perfumes, and opt for diluted essential oils instead. Look for alternatives to products in unnecessary packaging.

28. Green sports

If you're into resource-hungry sports, why not switch to activities that have far less impact on the planet?

The message is loud and clear: we should all be doing sport, and lots of it. Well, that's a no brainer, but there's no getting away from the fact that some sports eat up large tracts of land and water, disturb wildlife or spew harmful emissions into the air.

Skiing, for one, has a huge impact on the planet. Mountains are torn apart to open up the wide runs favoured by skiers, and roads are bulldozed into the hills. Customers fly or drive in, often in large SUVs. Increasingly the snow is less than satisfactory, and has to be created using chemicals and electricity. Energy is used in huge quantities to carry skiers up slopes, only for them to slide back down again!

Here's an idea for you

Walking is environmentally friendly and you could start today. Walking is low impact in all senses: it uses minimal resources, doesn't cost a penny and is gentle enough to suit all abilities. It's good for your heart, lungs, muscles and bone growth, and your feeling of wellbeing.

Defining idea

'I have two doctors, my left leg and my right.'
GEORGE TREVELYAN

Of course it's not just skiing that has an impact on the planet. Anything with an engine – motor racing, jet skiing, dirtbike riding, power boating – is less than green, not to mention noisy. Even sports such as football and athletics that are inherently harmless cause major environmental effects thanks to the transport of spectators, the litter they produce and the power required for the stadiums. Gyms are pretty greedy, too: they gobble huge amounts of energy to power the machines and air conditioning and heat the halls and pools.

Of course, there are many sports and activities that don't eat up land and water or belch emissions into the atmosphere: cycling, yoga, Pilates, horse riding, martial arts, swimming in the sea, rivers or lakes, jogging and many team sports.

But the ultimate in sustainability could be green gyms – eco-friendly, cheaper alternatives to traditional health clubs. Members 'work out' outdoors, burning off all that energy in conservation activities, such as planting trees, dry stone walling or creating school nature areas. No special experience or kit is required. And best of all – unlike your local gym – it's free. To join a group, or even start your own, visit btcv.org.uk or greengym.org.uk.

29. Pets count too

You can reduce your pets' carbon paw-prints, and keep them happy and healthy at the same time.

Many people love the idea of a cute, cuddly kitten or puppy. But before you head for the breeder, think about whether you could offer a home to an unwanted pet. Tens of thousands of dogs and cats are dumped each year, so why not visit an animal rescue centre, and choose a pet who needs a home?

Once your furry friend is established, buy it toys made from recycled materials or sustainable fibres such as hemp. These days, you can even get pet beds made with organic cotton or recycled PET bottles. Scrap yarn and fabric can easily be transformed into pet toys with some basic crafty know-how. And they won't have had to be trucked thousands of miles just to get slobbered on.

Here's an idea for you

When your pet dies, how will you dispose of it thoughtfully? There are green burial and cremation options for pets as well as for humans, so seek them out. And don't flush fish down the loo, even if they're dead, as they can spread disease.

Pets can contribute to noise pollution – dogs in particular. Often this is simply down to boredom so ensure your dog has a stimulating environment and don't leave it alone for too long. Then there's the impact pets can have on wildlife. Keep your cat indoors at night when it is likely to hunt. You might also consider putting bells around its collar – the sonic variety are most effective in alerting birds.

Natural and organic pet foods use meats that are raised in sustainable, humane ways without added drugs or hormones. Certified-organic pet food is pricier than the standard variety, but worth it if you consider that it is meeting strict standards that spell out how ingredients are produced and processed. If you feel strongly about it, there is no reason why your dog can't have a meat-free diet, although cats can't be veggies without supplements.

Most of our pets' poop winds up in a landfill, where it's embalmed in plastic bags. You can compost the poop, but not in your usual compost pile, as it doesn't reach high enough temperatures to kill pathogens, which could in turn reach your home-grown produce. If you bury an old bin a safe distance away from your vegetable garden, you can use it as dedicated a pet-waste composter.

30. The home farm

What could be nicer than eating organic, free-range eggs that were freshly laid just minutes ago in your own backyard?

As the eco-movement gathers momentum, there's been a huge surge of interest in growing your own, and that includes rearing pigs, chickens, ducks and bees. Keeping your own puts you in touch with the whole process of rearing, and possibly slaughtering, livestock. They can lend a hoof in the garden, too – pigs will root around, clearing and fertilising ground ready for planting, chickens will peck away at soil pests and apply a light coating of manure to a cleared vegetable bed, bees will provide free pollination services and ducks will eat your slugs.

Given the size of most people's properties, chickens are probably the most straightforward choice as garden livestock: they are unobtrusive, don't smell and aren't noisy. Chickens need sturdy housing to protect them from foxes, and a grass-based run on

Here's an idea for you

If your neighbours seem disapproving of the new additions to your family, invite them to meet them – chances are they'll be charmed. Offer them a share of the eggs, or the odd jar of honey, and they'll soon come round.

which they can be 'rotated' so they always have access to a fresh, clean patch. Depending on the breed, each hen can produce 100–300 eggs per year, so if you and your family are seriously into eggs you may need a few chickens.

Ducks can also thrive in gardens, but they must have their own pond. They cost about as much to keep as chickens. Ducks do have one distinct advantage for any organic gardener: they eat slugs.

Perhaps surprisingly, bees make very good urban livestock, partly due to the large variety of plants and flowers you find in cities. Their honey is full of minerals and natural compounds, and can be scoffed on organic bread, in tea or coffee, or made into mead. The beeswax can be used for candles.

At the top end of the urban livestock scale are pigs. They need at least 35 square metres per pig, preferably more. As they are intelligent, sociable animals, you need to allow enough room for a few. There are also rules about pig ownership, and your site may need to be assessed first. (An alternative is to 'outsource' pig keeping to someone like the Number One Pig Consortium (www.numberonepig.co.uk) who will raise the rare-breed pig of your choice and deliver it ready for the freezer.)

31. Garden green

Once you begin to garden organically, you will be protecting your very own little piece of the planet.

It doesn't much matter whether you're after a flower-filled garden worthy of a horticultural show or a piece of land that's strictly for fruit and veg, gardening without the use of pesticides and other chemicals brings its own challenges and rewards. Organic gardening aims to be sustainable, ensuring the land and its resources will be available for future generations.

Many gardeners agree that once you've got the hang of it, organic gardening is no harder than the conventional way. You'll also have the peace of mind of knowing exactly what has gone into your soil as well as the pleasure of seeing what comes out of it.

Here's an idea for you

Draw up a plan of your organic garden before you get planting, either on paper or using a garden design PC program. Having the design in front of you will help you incorporate plenty of variety, which is the key to the successful organic garden, and plan large features such as ponds or wild areas.

The starting point in organic gardening is to improve your soil. You can dig in or spread around organic matter such as leaf mould, composted bark and garden compost. You'll soon find their bulk

Defining idea

'Healthy soil creates healthy plants and healthy people.'
J.I. RODALE, organic pioneer

'When we heal the earth, we heal ourselves.'
DAVID ORR, ENVIRONMENTALIST

will improve the drainage of heavy soils and allow dry soil to hold onto moisture and nutrients. Make your own compost by filling a large compost bin with layers of prunings, peelings, egg shells, tea bags, old flower heads and even bits of cardboard for a nutrient rich compost.

You don't need a strong weed killer – prevent growth with a carpet of bark mulch, leaf mould or composted straw across soil. Watch the soil like a hawk – if any weeds do dare to show their faces, pull them up or hoe them before they have a chance to set seed.

Get to know your soil type and buy plants that suit it, and the position you put them in – strong plants are less likely to succumb to diseases or pests. Choose naturally disease-resistant varieties whenever you can.

All gardens have pests, but don't reach for a chemical spray when your plants come under attack, encourage natural predators instead. Hedgehogs and toads will scoff slugs and snails, while lacewings and ladybirds have a voracious appetite for greenfly. Install bug boxes and piles of stones or logs for creatures to hibernate in, and have some kind of water feature, even if it's only a tiny pond.

32. Low-water garden

Is your garden swallowing up more than its fair share of water? Help conserve water with drought-proof planting.

With fresh water supplies seriously under threat thanks to increased demand and global warming, every one of us has to cut back on how much water we use in times of drought, and that means in the garden, too. Luckily, water-efficient gardens can reduce your water bills and running costs; they require less maintenance and use the available space in the most practical way.

As with all things gardening related, the soil is the place to start – a healthy, well-maintained soil with plenty of organic matter will retain moisture and nutrients. If you're choosing new plants, make sure you look out for varieties that are drought tolerant, and plant them as early in the season as possible so they can grow deep roots before dry weather begins. You can reduce watering once the roots are established.

Here's an idea for you

Cut off the base of plastic bottles and bury them upside down next to new plants. Water into these and they'll channel the water straight to the roots.

Defining idea

'A garden is half made when it is well planned.'
LIBERTY HYDE BAILEY, horticulturist

Lawns are the thirstiest part of a garden. Letting the grass grow longer helps shade the soil and reduces the need for water. If you must water your lawn, remember that less frequent soaking is better than regular sprinkling as it encourages the roots to search for water stored deep below the soil's surface. Water in the early morning or in the evening to avoid evaporation.

Make sure your garden hose doesn't have any wasteful leaks, and fit it with a trigger to control the flow. An aerating nozzle allows you to water roots without washing away the soil or having to use the less efficient spray pattern.

Your best investment in case of drought is a water butt, or two if your garden is big enough – many water firms sell them cut price. A water butt (or underground tank) collects water run-off from roofs and gutters and provides vital water supplies when things dry up. Greywater from baths and showers can be used safely on most non-edible plants, provided it is applied to the soil rather than foliage and not left long enough for bacteria to grow.

33. Lovely compost

Homemade compost improves the soil, recycles organic matter and helps conserve water. And it's absolutely free!

The rules of compost making are pretty easy. If it can rot, it can compost, but some things like grass cuttings and soft young weeds break down quickly. They work as 'hotter rotters', or activators, getting the composting started, but on their own will decay to little more than a mushy mess. Older and tougher plant material is slower to rot but gives body to the finished compost. Woody items decay very slowly, so they are best chopped or shredded.

A good compost heap is like a good cake: light, moist and made up of layers! And like a cake, texture is key. When you start your compost bin or heap, choose a spot in the garden on well-drained, level ground. Fork the soil over lightly, then put a layer of scrunched up or shredded paper on the ground.

There are two types of material – 'green' (grass clippings, fruit and vegetable waste, soft weeds, etc) and 'brown' (e.g. cardboard, straw,

Here's an idea for you

If you want to get compost faster you will need at least a cubic metre of material which must be turned over frequently in a wooden container or open heap. It's a lot of work but you'll get the finished compost in around two months.

woody trimmings, old leaves) – which need to be added in roughly equal amounts. Add them chopped up and in light layers. If the material is very dense and compacted or very finely shredded, add some more scrunched up paper or ripped up cardboard to keep air pockets in the mix.

You can also add a few handfuls of soil, some well rotted compost from another heap or some horse manure. This will encourage the helpful micro-organisms to colonise your new heap quickly. To keep the heap moist and warm, cover it with an old piece of carpet or put a lid on it.

A good heap will start to heat up as the rotting process takes place. The hotter it is, the faster it rots and some heaps will reach 60°C if they are big enough and have the right materials in them. It can take up to a year for all the organic material to break down although you can add activators and composting worms (from your local garden centre) that will speed things up.

Some materials should be banned from your heap: meat, fish, coal/coke ash, cat litter, dog waste, disposable nappies and glossy magazines.

34. Grow your own

Whether you own a window box or a meadow, every outdoor space can yield a fine crop of organic fruit or veg.

Growing vegetables and fruit successfully is no different to growing any other plant. Start with good plants or seed, give them what they want – food, water and light – and they'll do the work for you. You don't need a huge plot either.

It doesn't have to be time-consuming or expensive to grow your own food. A few packets of seeds and some basic tools – a spade, fork, hoe, rake, trowel and watering can – will provide you with all you need to fill a plot with vegetables. As well as being fun, growing your own food is a healthy, productive and sustainable activity. You can involve the whole family: children will benefit enormously from learning where food comes from.

Here's an idea for you

If you've only got room for one crop this year, make it courgettes. They're prolific, a doddle to cultivate from either seed or plant, and can even be grown in a pot. Cooked as a vegetable (though technically a fruit), organically grown courgettes taste gorgeous and are a good source of vitamins A and C, potassium, antioxidants and fibre.

Defining idea

'The fruit derived from labour is the sweetest of pleasures.'
LUC DE VAUVENARGUES

When you're thinking about where to grow fruit and vegetables in your garden, try to find a sunny spot with good drainage and no overhanging branches. A south-facing aspect is ideal. Avoid areas next to hedges as they tend to be dry. Provide shelter from wind, and netting or chicken wire to give protection from wildlife such as birds and squirrels. Divide the plot into four areas – this enables you to rotate the crops and minimises disease problems.

There's room for a few organic fruit and vegetables in any garden, no matter how small. You can grow herbs and salads in window boxes, vegetables among ornamentals (or vice versa), or make the most of vertical spaces such as a runner bean 'hedge', or grow beans, gourds, cucumbers or melons over a willow teepee frame.

Lots of varieties are happy in pots or growing bags if you look after them well. You can buy ready-grown sweet pepper, courgettes, climbing beans, chilli pepper, cherry tomato, aubergine and strawberries, or try herbs or salad leaves grown from seed. For larger fruit bushes such as blueberries, figs, peaches and apricots, select a larger pot and make sure you check the compost requirements on the plant label.

35. The good – and green – companions

Fancy yourself as a bit of a matchmaker? Pairing up works for plants as well as people, so get plotting.

It worked for Greek and Roman gardeners, and thousands of years on it still works for their modern-day counterparts – companion planting is one of the simplest ways you can go organic. By grouping certain plants together you can use their natural properties to boost pest control and improve growth. Companion planting also fosters a deeper understanding of what it means to be an organic gardener.

For instance, a particular plant may add nutrients to the soil, or it may distract pests or lure beneficial insects. Others may protect delicate plants from the sun and wind. As gardeners, we can build thriving plant communities by giving each plant the right type of soil, shelter, aspect and treatment.

Here's an idea for you

If you're new to this, you can't get a better friend than nasturtiums. They can keep aphids, cabbage worms, Colorado beetles, squash bugs and whitefly at bay. To top that, their golden-orange flowers, leaves and pickled seeds can all be added into a mixed salad to give colour, flavour and texture.

Defining idea

'A garden is a grand teacher.'
GERTRUDE JEKYLL

Many plants attract bees and butterflies. By supporting insect populations plants increase the number of hard-working pollinators, predators and parasites that are a natural part of a healthy garden. Plants may also attract birds and other creatures that prey on pests and are generally beneficial. Many pests locate their food by smell, so combining strong-smelling plants such as marigolds with susceptible crops will cause confusion and reduce attacks. Other strongly scented deterrents include rosemary, thyme, sage, lavender, chives, wormwood and garlic.

Marigolds are also loved by hoverflies, which help keep down aphids. Other flowers that are rich in nectar and attract pest predators include echinacea, coreopsis and aster. Wild flowers also attract beneficial bugs so if you have the space, section off a corner of your garden.

Here are a few planting combinations that work. Asparagus contain a substance called asparagin that repels tomato pests. Carrots and leeks or onions can be planted together to protect against a number of pests: leeks repel carrot fly and carrots repel onion fly and leek moth. Camomile is known as the physician plant because it perks up anything planted in or around it. Yarrow boosts vigour in other plants and accumulates phosphorous, calcium and silica, which can benefit homemade compost. It attracts many beneficial creatures such as hoverflies and ladybirds.

36. Your own eco-park

Turn your back yard into a natural haven for helpful insects, birds, frogs and other welcome visitors.

Biodiversity may be under threat from urbanisation, but we can all do our bit for wildlife by creating small-scale nature reserves in back yards, gardens and balconies. Encouraging a wide range of different species is one of the most planet-friendly steps you can take, as it helps preserve the delicate balance of the local ecosystem, without which we simply could not survive.

The key to encouraging birds and beasts is variety, whether of structure, design or planting. So, experiment with lots of different shapes and species by all means, but bear in mind that your garden should work as a cohesive whole, with features linked together so that wildlife can move between them easily rather than having a series of isolated features. Having several different heights is important, both with

Here's an idea for you

When it comes to the flower borders, variety is the key. Choose plants that flower at different times throughout the year so there is a steady supply of nectar for bees and butterflies throughout the season.

Defining idea

*'Wildlife doesn't just need the wild –
it can thrive in our gardens too.'*
**DAVID BELLAMY, botanist and
broadcaster**

physical structures (fences, sheds etc.)
and planting (climbers and shrubs).

One of the best ways of encouraging
wildlife into a garden is to add a
water feature, anything from a buried
old bowl to a designer wildlife pond.
Water will encourage frogs, hedgehogs and other wildlife that will feed
on bugs and snails. Birds will visit to drink and bathe. If you have room
for a pond, site it in a sunny position away from overhanging trees and
ensure the sides are slightly sloping, so birds can access it, amphibians
can spawn and hedgehogs can escape if they fall in.

Try leaving part of your lawn uncut to create a habitat for
grasshoppers, beetles and young amphibians, and provide roosts for
insects such as damselflies. Include some wildflowers to add interest
and more wildlife value.

Dead wood can be used to create a simple wood pile or interesting
sculptural feature, and is a useful habitat for lots of different
invertebrates. A pile of stones does a similar job, too. You can also
easily help wildlife with features such as bird and bat boxes, solitary
bee nests and bird feeders. Birds can be provided with food, either
bought seed or food scraps, throughout the year.

37. From day one

Start your kids off with a green and healthy lifestyle, and they'll take good habits into their own adulthood.

You love your kids, right? So show it in the way you all live, from nappies onwards. Kids learn from their parents, so teach them about our fragile planet right from the beginning. Luckily the choices you make for your children in terms of sustainability are often also healthier and more fun. The downside is that organic food and cotton, certified wooden furniture and eco-tourism can be pricier than their standard equivalents. Still, as parents you can't put a price on your kids, just as you can't put a price on the planet's wellbeing.

But going green is not only about buying the 'right' products for your kids – it's also about what you don't buy. The alarming battery of equipment forced onto new mums is only the start, to be followed by mountains of plastic toys and later by gadgets that eat up electricity and keep the kids indoors. So, buy the minimum, and maintain some healthy cynicism about bandwagons like 'eco' baby products.

Here's an idea for you

Save cash and reduce your home's plastic pile-up by joining a toy library. Toy libraries provide good quality educational and play items for loan, plus DVDs, CDs and even computer games.

Defining idea

'Wrinkles are hereditary. Parents get them from their children.'
DORIS DAY

There are other ways than shopping yourself green. Get your children in touch with their planet – perhaps give them their own patch of garden to look after, or let them help you gather or prepare food so they become aware of its origins. As part of the daily routine, teach them to turn off lights and appliances when not in use, recycle leftovers, pick up litter and walk or cycle, rather than drive.

Another way is to cut down on chemicals in your home. Research shows that small children are more vulnerable to the harmful effects of toxins, so reduce cleaning products, antibacterials, PVC products and fire-retarded furnishings, all of which can contain potentially harmful chemicals.

When your baby gets older, you can shop for organic baby food or, better still, make your own from fresh organic ingredients. That way you can prioritise locally produced, pesticide-free food, and get your child into good eating habits right from the start.

38. Lighten up

Maximise the use of natural light in your home, and make artificial lighting as energy-wise as you can.

Not only are the stars are being blotted out by man-made light pollution, but too much unnecessary artificial light also harms the environment by wasting valuable energy. In addition, many birds and animals are affected by stray light intruding into their night world, confusing their natural patterns, deterring them from established foraging areas, and affecting their breeding cycles. So it makes sense to limit the amount we use and make the most of natural light.

To maximise the natural light in your home, the first thing you can do is let light come through windows without interruptions. Remove objects from window sills and keep curtains out of the way. Place a large mirror opposite the window to reflect light around the room. Choose light and bright paint colours to reflect light. Choose a

Here's an idea for you

Natural daylight is completely free and imparts warmth and energy into any room. Make the most of it by keeping your windows as clear as possible. Fit over-width curtain rails so that the curtains can be pulled right to the sides and don't block out those valuable rays.

Defining idea

'A nocturnal world without escape
from the glare of electrical lights is
disturbing.'
PHILIP J. DEVRIES, biologist

pale flooring for the same reason –
glossy surfaces such as polished
wood reflect more light than soft,
absorbent ones like carpet.

One way to be more energy
efficient with artificial lighting is to
use more compact fluorescent lamps (CFLs) in the home. No longer
associated with drab factory settings, today's CFLs are high-quality
lamps with good visual properties. An old-fashioned (incandescent)
bulb converts only 5% of the energy into light. A CFL converts
around 25% of the energy into light. The next generation of lighting
is being based on light-emitting diodes. These are around 70%
efficient, and they will probably get better.

Security lighting is hugely wasteful and can even be antisocial when
the angle and position of the lights is inappropriate. Always start by
asking if the lighting is necessary, or could the desired security be
achieved with prickly foliage or screening? If lights are the answer,
you don't need the 500W monsters; a 150W lamp is adequate for
domestic purposes. Make sure that lights are adjusted to illuminate
the area intended and not neighbouring property. For an all-night
porch light a 9W lamp is perfectly OK.

39. The greener PC

In our mad rush to upgrade all things electronic, it's easy to forget how resource-hungry computers can be.

Most Western households now have at least one PC, but just how sustainable is this valuable piece of hardware? Research by the UN into the environmental impact of computers found that around 1.8 tonnes of raw material are needed to manufacture the average desktop PC and monitor. Environmental issues also surround the peripherals and handheld gadgets, not to mention mobile phones.

The UN report concluded that the best way to minimise the impact on the environment of a PC is to extend its useful life by, for instance, turning off equipment when it is not being used and cutting down on printing. You could also upgrade the memory or hard disk space as much a possible, and use accessories such as a USB wireless stick – a small plug-in that can provide fast wi-fi access. Strip your software down to the essentials – don't use valuable space or

Here's an idea for you

Assess manufacturers' green credentials by checking out the Green Electronics Guide on the Greenpeace website (www.greenpeace.org), which ranks leading PC and mobile suppliers on their global policies regarding use of toxic chemicals and disposal of the electronic waste generated by their products.

processor memory on programs
and files you don't use.

Remember that equipment that is
beyond its useful life for you may
be of use to someone else. It can be
refurbished and passed on to schools, charities or other individuals.
If hardware fails completely, it must be disposed of carefully as most
of it contains harmful or toxic elements and should not be thrown
in a skip. The European Union's WEEE Directive (Waste Electrical
and Electronic Equipment, www.weeeman.org) is now enforcing the
safe disposal of electronic equipment. Ask your local authority for
info.

If you're buying new, there is no reason why you can't get your
hands on a relatively ethical piece of hardware. You'll need to take
into account the environmental impact of the manufacturing
process, any specific energy-saving features and how easily the
computer can be recycled when you've done with it.

Some companies are producing 'carbon neutral' PCs, eliminating
toxins from their computers such as PVC and brominated flame
retardants (BFRs), using recycled components and carbon offsetting,
planting trees to offset the power used to run the computers and
offering to recycle any unwanted hardware.

40. Four wheels bad

If you can't do without your motor, at least take a few sensible measures to reduce pollution.

While Hollywood celebs seem to be embracing the new breed of eco-cars, the rest of us are rather trailing behind. A hybrid or electric car may be too expensive or not suit our day-to-day needs for various reasons, but there are still things we can look out for when buying a new car. The most obvious route is to choose the smallest and most fuel-efficient vehicle possible. This will also save money in road tax and other running costs. Look for one with the lowest CO_2 emissions of its class and which meets the new Euro IV standard.

Many new car makers are giving plenty of useful information to help you make your choice, such as eco labels that show CO_2 emission figures and estimated annual running costs, and possibly even provide life-cycle assessment, which examines the whole impact of the vehicle from factory to final disposal.

Here's an idea for you

If you live in a city, why not sell your car and join a car club instead? It's a brilliant way of cutting emissions and will save you loads in running costs as well. You only hire the car when you need it, and this can be by the hour, week, month or longer.

Another idea to investigate is running your car on liquid petroleum gas (LPG), which produces much lower emissions – about 10% to 15% less CO_2, 75% less carbon monoxide and 85% less hydrocarbons – and is much cheaper than unleaded petrol.

The way you drive your car also has an impact on the environment. If you're eco-savvy, emissions and fuel consumption can be reduced by up to 25%. Restarting the engine uses less energy than ten seconds of idling, so switch off if in a long queue. Use higher gears as soon as traffic conditions allow. Minimum emissions happen between 40–60 miles per hour and increase when you drive faster. Regular maintenance will reduce emissions. Hard acceleration and sharp breaking will use more fuel.

When the engine is cold, journeys of less than 2 miles pollute by up to 60% more per mile than a hot engine so walk or take public transport whenever you can. Make sure your tyres are inflated to the right pressure and reduce greenhouse gas emissions by 5%.

41. Green at work

You're bound to spend several hours a day at work, so why not make your workplace as green as you can?

Whether you work alone at home or with a group of people in a large organisation, the way your office is run can have a massive impact on the environment. Even doing simple things that cost little or nothing can help face up to the big problems of the greenhouse effect and climate change.

As well as eco-unfriendly heating and air conditioning, most offices today possess an army of electronic equipment such as photocopiers, printers and computers, which are essential but use up loads of electricity. Save energy (and the planet!) by making sure all equipment is switched off at night. (An average-size photocopier left on overnight wastes enough energy to make thousands of copies.) And turn down the heating – if your workplace heating system has thermostatic valves on radiators, use them.

Here's an idea for you

Don't chuck out your empties! Around 90% of used-up ink and toner cartridges can be refilled up to eight or ten times, so don't simply bin them when they get to the end of their printing life.

99

Defining idea

'Inspiration comes of working every day.'
CHARLES BAUDELAIRE

Remember the three Rs: by reducing, reusing and recycling waste from the office we can save money, natural resources and energy. Reduce by using your own mug or glass rather than plastic or polystyrene cups for drinks; use e-mail rather than paper messages. When printing draft copies, use scrap paper. Reuse envelopes for internal circulation and buy envelope reuse labels. Be scrupulous about recycling glass, paper, plastic, metal and other materials. Ask the local authority for advice if necessary.

Many offices buy and use far more than they actually need, meaning that more resources are consumed than is necessary. There is a lot that can be done to cut down what is bought and to use what we have more efficiently. Lobby for more thoughtful purchasing by your organisation.

There are other things you can do to work in a more eco-responsible way. Take the stairs rather than the lift – it's healthier and reduces energy use. Invest in solar powered calculators rather than battery operated. Avoid disposable products in favour of reuseable items: china cups, metal cutlery, propelling pencils, refillable pens.

42. A clean break

As spending on eco-tourism increases, so do some travel firms' claims to sustainability. Make sure you avoid the 'greenwash'.

We've all heard the term 'eco-tourism' bandied about, but not everyone knows exactly what it means. It is generally agreed nowadays that eco-tourism – or sustainable tourism – involves travelling responsibly to regions in a way that helps protect the environment and benefits the lifestyle of the local people.

Eco-tourism can encompass a wide range of features, but you would probably expect it to include accommodation built from local, preferably recycled, materials, fairly-paid staff from the immediate area, energy from renewable sources where possible, and water-saving policies. Eco holidays should have no impact on the natural environment, and help maintain traditional cultures and customs.

Here's an idea for you

Why not give the beach a miss this year and opt for a conservation break instead? From landscape restoration in Transylvania through wildlife management in Botswana to tree planting in Nepal, there is a project worldwide to suit everyone.

Defining idea

'*Who lives sees much. Who travels sees more.*'
Arab proverb

It's not eco-tourism if the resort café simply has Fairtrade coffee, includes visits to the homes of the locals, or uses solar power. What you need to look out for are wide-ranging measures that cover the whole experience. There are hotels, for instance, which are furnished in almost 100% recycled material, and invest in efficient technologies that minimise their use of electricity and water. Other travel operators work alongside welfare or conservation charities that benefit local communities directly.

While you can obviously form your own judgement of a company, it would be helpful if there was an international form of classification – an eco-friendliness star-rating system for travel firms are. Sadly, as yet there isn't. However, there are some internet-based pathbreakers on this: Green Globe (www.greenglobe.org), a global benchmarking, certification and improvement system for sustainable travel and tourism; The Travel Foundation (www.thetravelfoundation.org.uk) provides a handy list of the many ways individuals can travel more responsibly; and www.responsibletravel.com provides a good overview of the issues involved and offers a wide range of ecotourism holidays, from holistic centres in the Greek islands to wildlife tours in the Antarctic.

43. Low-impact travel

Wherever you travel, tread lightly. If you behave responsibly, you will minimise your impact on the local environment.

No matter where your travels take you this year, travelling responsibly maximises the benefits and minimises the negative effects of tourism. Start thinking 'low impact' before you go, even if you're not travelling abroad. Plan your route to minimise carbon emissions – go by train rather than driving or flying. For the flights that you can't avoid, offset the carbon emissions through one of the many carbon balancing scheme.

Show respect for other people's culture and customs. Ask permission before you take photos of people or sensitive buildings. Be careful not to disturb ruins and historic sites and don't be tempted to collect wild plants, rocks, shells etc. If you hire a local guide you'll discover more about local culture and lives, and they will earn an income. Use public transport, hire a bike or walk when convenient – it's a great way to meet local people on their terms and reduce pollution and carbon emissions.

Here's an idea for you

Get into the habit of taking a recycled plastic bag for collecting your litter wherever you travel. Our throw-away society has led to a massive increase in litter, and as well as ruining the landscape it is a menace to wildlife.

Defining idea

'Take only photos, leave only footprints.'
Popular saying

In many destinations, resources such as water and energy are precious and local people may not have enough for their own needs. Help out by turning off (or down) heating/air conditioning, lights and the TV when you're not using them. Let hotel staff know if you are happy to reuse towels and bed linen rather having them replaced daily. Be aware of how much water you are using. If you have to wash in streams or rivers, don't use detergents or other chemicals – go for an eco soap instead.

Discover the beauty of the natural environment but take special care not to damage the landscape, plants and trees that are the homes and food for wildlife. In fields where crops are growing, follow paths wherever you can. Be aware that hotter and drier weather conditions make wildfires a problem, and they can obviously be devastating to wildlife and habitats as well as to people and property. Don't drop matches or cigarette ends and if you're planning a barbecue, make sure you have it in a designated area and be sure to extinguish it carefully.

44. Money matters

Carry out a financial health check: could your money be doing better ethically? Don't let profit overrule your principles.

Ethical financial products have been around in various guises for many years, and recently they have been extended to include bank accounts, insurance policies, pensions and mortgages offering environmental benefits.

However, ethical (or socially responsible) investment can be very confusing as there are so many different funds available that claim to be 'green'. In reality some of these funds are more environmentally friendly than others. You can find out which UK or global companies have ethical policies by simply reading information readily found on their websites or company literature.

Here's an idea for you

As the green agenda grows stronger, eco-friendly companies will become ever more attractive to investors. So, to invest ethically, put your money into firms and products that promote sustainability and offset carbon etc. – e.g. mortgage deals based on how ecologically sound/energy efficient your home is.

Broadly speaking, a truly ethical company will be one that is not causing damage to the environment, not exploiting its workforce by paying low wages, not using child labour, and not producing products that are harmful or dangerous. The negative criteria identifying companies to steer clear of are such things as poor disposal of hazardous waste, testing on animals, or involvement in supporting oppressive regimes.

Criteria like these are not necessarily failsafe, and certainly not tailor-made to your particular set of beliefs. For instance, you might be attracted to investing in a biotechnology company that is carrying out ground-breaking research into tuberculosis but is also involved in the genetically modified foods you might shy away from. You have to decide how to prioritise your principles otherwise you may end up not investing in any companies at all!

As the World Trade Organisation begins to crack down on companies exploiting people, animals or the environment, bad-boy companies will receive negative press and lose customers, meaning they'll start to underperform. Well-run companies with strong ethical principles should be tomorrow's top performers, along with the many companies producing sustainable energy products. So, think long term when you're investing your money.

45. Outside the box

From mosquito nets to goats, your ethical gift to friends and family could have global benefits.

Christmas, birthdays, Mother's Day, Valentine's … it all adds up to one thing: lots and lots of present buying. Do we have more money than sense? Sometimes it seems so. Think of all the trash around that is loosely classed as 'gifts'. And, all too often, they end up simply shoved into the back of a cupboard. Now's the time to ditch the wasteful tat and turn instead to gifts that have more long-term benefit to communities and the planet.

There are hundreds of shops and websites dedicated to eco gifts made from organic cotton, recycled materials and Fairtrade products, but sometimes it's nice to offer something a bit different. As well as successful high-street shops, charities such as Oxfam run online stores where instead of buying a tangible present you pay

Here's an idea for you

Kids might not be impressed with a certificate for a goat they don't get to see. However, there are still green options you can turn to. Be ultra-practical and buy a solar-powered iPod re-charger or an LED torch, ethically made fashion accessories or funky wind-up radios. Simpler still, Fairtrade chocolate or cotton products such as T-shirts.

Defining idea

'I feel more confident than ever that the power to save the planet rests with the individual consumer.'
DENIS HAYES, environmental activist

for something that goes to a developing community, while the recipient of your 'gift' gets a certificate or card that represents the gift.

You can pay for an animal such as a donkey, a goat or a yak, a series of school dinners, saplings and food growing packs. The more generous can splash out on new toilet facilities, allotments, or a whole mango plantation! You could also buy membership to an eco charity, such as the Soil Association, or give a gift of a climate relief pack.

From whales to dormice, there's an endangered animal out there that needs your sponsorship. Adopters normally receive a gift pack containing an adoption certificate, a fact sheet about the animal, and sometimes a soft toy version. Most wildlife charities offer this service, and it's especially good for kids.

It can be tempting to splurge on cards and wrapping paper, but it doesn't do the planet any favours – that giftwrap was once a tree! Find giftwrap made from recycled paper, and reuse your own. Greenest of all, dispense with wrapping paper altogether: hide presents and turn the giving process into a treasure hunt or wrap the gift in a pretty scarf or fabric offcut.

46. Way to go

Funerals: they have to happen, and they can be eco-friendly. Be bold and plan ahead for the inevitable.

It may seem ghoulish to be planning funerals in advance, but a growing number of people, young and old, are hoping for an eco-friendly death rather than a final swipe at the environment. After all, if caring about the environment is an important part of your life, what could be more fitting than an ending that embraces the natural cycle of death, decay and new growth?

The high cost of burial plots has made cremation a cheaper and more attractive option. However, there is a not-so-green side to cremation. As well as wasting large amounts of energy and timber, when wooden coffins are burned they release dioxin, acids and sulphur dioxide into the atmosphere. One green step you can take is to go for a cardboard coffin. Most crematoriums now accept these and some even offer a discount as less energy is used.

Here's an idea for you

It's worth drawing up your own eco-funeral plan now. This will ensure you get exactly what you want, and will also help you budget – you'll be paying at today's prices! Make sure any money you pay is underwritten.

Burial can be a greener option, so long as you go about it the right way, for instance in choosing the right coffin. Regular coffins contain formaldehyde that soaks into the ground over time. There are a number of eco designs on the market made from natural materials without harmful chemicals, such as biodegradable papier mache (made out of recycled paper), bamboo, wicker, seagrass and willow.

If you've opted for burial and chosen your coffin, the next step is to choose a location. Urban cemeteries are running out of space, which means that managed woodland burial sites are becoming increasingly popular. These sites are kept as natural and wild as possible in order to promote biodiversity, and the land is preserved from development. To avoid polluting the ground with harmful chemicals, bodies buried in natural sites are not embalmed. Graves are usually unmarked, although a memorial tree or wildflowers can take the place of a headstone.

A key attraction of a funeral at a natural burial ground is the freedom offered to choose the format of the service. They are suitable for the religious and the secular alike, and the mourners can take all the time they need to say goodbye.

47. Fellow greens

Feeling green but lonely? Don't fret: there will be loads of like-minded people in your area – you just have to find them.

Warning: turning eco is highly addictive. Once the green bug bites, you'll want to get into the whole environmental thing in more depth, meeting other like-minded eco-'worriers', finding out more information and discovering how your local community is helping to change things.

The first thing you could do is nip down to your local library or log on to your local authority's website and find out if there are any environmental groups in your neighbourhood. These could be anything from local conservation volunteers to hardline campaigners – it's up to you how far you want to go.

Here's an idea for you

Try arranging a swap party – the eco-friendly way to get new stuff without being a consumer. Your like-minded guests bring things along that they don't want any more – software, CDs, tools, books – and the other guests can take their pick of anything they want. The leftovers can be donated to charity.

For instance, you could get in touch with an organisation, such as British Trust for Conservation Volunteers, that runs regular day

Defining idea

'If we do not change our direction, we are likely to end up where we are headed.'
Chinese Proverb

conservation tasks all over the country, during the week and at weekends. There is sure to be a branch near you, and you can join in whenever you wish. There's no need to book in advance – just turn up at the meeting point on the day.

Tasks vary from tree planting to dry stone walling, footpath construction to creating wildlife habitats. You don't need to be an eco-expert either – project leaders will show you the ropes and you're free to work at your own pace. You'll make new friends, get some fresh air, exercise and help your local environment.

You could also find out if there are any carbon rationing action groups in your area. This network has members in many towns and villages. The aim of each group is to cap carbon use and compensate for excess emissions by paying into a fund for energy-saving causes. Focusing on just one or two measures – for example, heating, electricity, car usage – the groups help members calculate their individual carbon footprints, and agree targets.

Apart from helping you get your carbon footprint down, it's a marvellous way of meeting new people and widening your knowledge of the whole climate change topic. Often groups invite expert guests along to talk about their specialist field.

48. Low-carb diet

We've all got one, and most of us have got an oversize one. Yes, our carbon footprint shows just how green we really are.

A couple of years ago few had even heard the phrase carbon footprint. But now we're all fast becoming carbon literate, if not yet neutral. A carbon footprint is the measure of the total amount of greenhouse gases released into the atmosphere as a result of things we do in our everyday lives.

Your footprint is made up of the primary footprint, a measure of our direct emissions of CO_2 from the burning of fossil fuels (for heating and transport), and the secondary footprint, which measures indirect CO_2 emissions from the whole life-cycle of the products we use, from manufacture through to eventual breakdown.

A carbon footprint is measured in tonnes per year, and the sustainable level for every person on the planet has been estimated at one tonne per person. Given national averages of 3.2 tonnes for China, 11 tonnes for the UK and 20

Here's an idea for you

If you want to get into carbon offsetting, make sure the offset provider conforms to the government's gold standard (see www.cdmgoldstandard.org). This conforms to the Kyoto protocol on climate change.

Defining idea

'*Before you finish eating your breakfast this morning you've depended on half the world.*'
MARTIN LUTHER KING, JR.

tonnes for the US, you can see that we're in trouble! There are numerous websites to help you work out your footprint, such as www.carbonneutral.com and www.carbonfootprint.com.

But everyone can cut their carbon footprint. Although individual actions can't possibly solve the problem, every little helps. For instance, you could save 2 kg of carbon for every journey under three miles where you walk and don't use the car, and 30 kg by switching the power off in your house at night. To shrink your primary footprint, don't go by air, sign up to a renewable energy provider, insulate and install solar water heating, car share and use public transport. Reduce your secondary footprint by avoiding items that produce high emissions during manufacture or delivery (e.g. don't buy bottled water from abroad; don't buy food from the other side of the world – buy local or grow your own; give red meat a miss; shun highly packaged items).

A carbon offset provider can calculate the emissions you produce and then pay for them through a donation to a project that reduces carbon by the equivalent amount. However, this is not a panacea. Long term we need to radically cut our emissions rather than mitigate them.

49. Cash, now!

Creating a sustainable planet for the future will cost a lot of money. You can do your bit by doing some fund-raising.

There are hundreds of different ecological campaign groups out there, and they tend to have one thing in common: money – or, rather, a lack of it. It takes massive resources to do the work that many of them set out to do, whether it's protecting endangered animal species, research into climate change, or planting new areas of rainforest. Many organisations rely on donations, so any contribution you can make is more than welcome.

Of course donating what you can, when you can is great, but you could take it a step further and actively raise money for the eco project of your choice.

Some of the best ideas are the simplest. For instance a sponsored walk or bike ride. Or give up something you would really miss, like chocolate, meat, beer or TV and get people to sponsor you for each day that you manage to go

Here's an idea for you

Once you've set aside what you want for family and friends, making a will is a good opportunity to make a donation to your favourite charity. And in most cases it should be exempt from tax! Ask your solicitor to help you draw it up.

Defining idea

'The gap in our economy is between what we have and what we think we ought to have.'
PAUL HEYNE, economist

without. Simple ideas are easy to follow through and also fit another top tip for fund-raisers – they cost next to nothing.

Get the kids involved too. Ask them to help neighbours with small tasks such as car washing, shopping or dog walking in return for donations, or get them to hold a sponsored silence, cake sale, recycled-fashion show, disco or other event at their school. The possibilities are almost endless: quizzes, raffles, bring-and-buy sales. However, don't forget to check whether there are any possible grants on offer from your local council and find out about matched funding from your employers.

Put another iron in the fire by creating your own fund-raising web page, and watch your donations grow. Global organisations such as World Land Trust and Friends of the Earth can help you raise money online through your sponsored efforts. Using a simple template, you choose a web address for your page, write a title and a message and add a photo if you like. You can then email the address of your page to everyone you know, anywhere in the world. They donate online by credit or debit card and the money you raise is paid into your chosen charity's bank account.

50. Green adventure

Swap theme parks for green parks. Take the kids on a day out where the only energy you burn is your own.

Days out with the kids always seem to involve long, hot journeys in cars, which mysteriously end up full of fast food cartons, sweet wrappers and empty plastic water bottles. It doesn't have to be that way. For a start, you could go by train, which is far more eco-friendly than the car, plus you'll probably get to see more of the countryside and with family travel discounts it can end up being cheaper, too.

You could even just walk or cycle somewhere local. Even the smallest or quietest neighbourhood has its eco secrets to reveal, whether it's an ancient pond full of fascinating creatures or a patch of long grass where you can hunt for mini beasts.

If you have a park near you, why not take them pond dipping? You don't need lots of special equipment, just a small net or glass jar. The most important tools you can have are your eyes – sit or stand

Here's an idea for you

Take the kids to see where food really comes from with a trip to a working organic farm. They'll be able to watch (and maybe even help with) cows being milked, eggs collected and crops planted or harvested. Younger children may be able to feed piglets, goats and lambs.

Defining idea

'We share the earth not only with our fellow human beings, but with all the other creatures.'
DALAI LAMA

still beside your wildlife pond and just watch. You will be amazed what you can see – frogs and newts rising to the surface, animals coming to the pond to drink, and colourful damsel flies swooping over the pond.

Sweep your nets through long grass a few times and then examine what you have caught before releasing them. Expect to find mini beasts like ladybirds, moths, dragonflies, butterflies, grasshoppers and caterpillars.

Younger children enjoy having a simple task, so set them a list of ten things you're likely to come across on a local nature trail. Include easy-to-spot wildflowers, leaf skeletons, empty snail shells, and seeds from the trees. You don't have to take what you find – you can just tick them off the list or snap them on a camera.

Of course there are endless alternative technology centres, biodomes, wildlife centres and the like to visit, but you can create your own agenda. It's good for children to learn that a great day out doesn't have to involve huge sums of money. And, in fact, some of the nicest places are absolutely free!

51. Party the eco way

If you're celebrating, why not spread the message by throwing a party that's environmentally friendly?

Whether you're hosting a wedding for hundreds or a small, exclusive dinner party, your celebration's green credentials don't just stop at the salads.

First off, choose the location. Have your party at home if there's room and it's convenient to others, but otherwise choose a venue close to where the majority of your guests live to cut down on the environmental costs associated with travel. Support a location or a non-profit organisation dedicated to green causes – parks, museums, or wildlife centres, for instance. Encourage your guests to come by public transport, or help them with car sharing rotas.

Here's an idea for you

Cut down on electricity and create a romantic and flattering glow at your party by placing lit candles everywhere. Use soy or beeswax candles, which, unlike petroleum-based paraffin candles, won't emit toxic, sooty fumes. Or get your hands on some plug-in LED lighting, which comes in pretty colours and is very energy efficient.

Next, you'll be sending out invites, so skip the pretty paper variety and choose e-cards as a more ecologically sound option. Or, if you prefer to commit yourself to paper, make it the recycled kind.

Now, the menu. Don't be tempted to fill up a trolley at the nearest cash and carry. Instead, visit a local organic farm or farmer's market to stock up on pesticide- and fertiliser-free goodies. Buying local products also means they've had to travel only a short distance (versus thousands of miles) to get to your house – which obviously means fewer freighting miles.

If you're on a tight budget, try to prepare most of the food yourself instead of buying ready-made, heavily packaged snacks. Rope in friends and family to help if cooking isn't your thing, or just keep it really simple. Finger food is ideal as it cuts out the need for crockery and cutlery – so no washing up! Hire glasses from supermarkets or wine merchants instead of using plastic ones.

Use your imagination when it comes to odds and ends that will add a finishing touch to your décor: check out markets and charity shops for centre pieces, table decorations and place mats. You may well get something unique and do your part to create less trash.

52. Eureco!

Yes, the planet's not well, but with TLC from people like you there's hope. Go on – go green for good.

Even the least media-savvy individual must now be aware that planet Earth is in a bit of a mess. And most of us are waking up to the fact that it's not going to get better on its own. The message is getting through loud and clear: *we all need to do something – now*. Many of us are now taking steps such as saving energy but could we be doing more?

We have become nations of shopaholics, bombarded by advertising which persuades us that the more we consume, the better our lives will be. But our obsessive consumerism is putting enormous pressure on the planet. It simply may not be enough to buy more carefully – what it probably comes down to is buying less. Imagine what will happen when a billion more people become consumers with the same spending power as the West?

Here's an idea for you

If you don't think the politicians are doing enough, get pestering! Write a letter, send an email or join a campaign. Friends of the Earth's 'Big Ask' initiative helps you get in touch with the relevant politicians and provides an email template. Get stuck in on the issues that fire you up.

Defining ideas

'Only when the last tree has died and the last river been poisoned and the last fish been caught will we realise we cannot eat money.'
Cree Indian Proverb

'The future belongs to those who prepare for it today.'
MALCOLM X

OK, buying less is the aim, but, when you do shop, buy more carefully. Learn what labels mean: for instance you've got Fairtrade, low-energy logos, organic certification, Forest Stewardship labels and the European Ecolabel, the flower symbol awarded to goods and services which meet strict criteria to minimise the impacts of consumer products on the environment.

It's not just about climate change: pollution is also a big factor. Try to reduce your 'toxic splash' – the number of synthetic chemicals in toiletries and cleaning products flushed down plugholes every day. These chemicals run into our water system and can damage our health and environment. Find out more at www.chemicalsafeskincare.co.uk.

One of the most important mantras to someone who cares about the planet is 'reduce, reuse, recycle'. Reduce unnecessary waste by avoiding pointless purchases. Buy products that can be reused, to reduce waste. Buy products with minimal packaging. Think before you throw away – many items that you would normally consider as rubbish could be used for other purposes or recycled.

Brilliant resources

Action/information groups
www.foe.org.uk
www.icount.org.uk
www.greenpeace.org
www.lightpollution.org.uk
www.stopclimatechaos.org
www.toxicsplash.co.uk
www.wen.org.uk
www.wwf.org

Cars
www.lowcvp.org.uk
www.vcacarfueldata.org.uk

Conservation
www2.btcv.org.uk
www.earthwatch.org
www.mcsuk.org
www.rainforestfoundationuk.org
www.wildlifetrusts.org
www.worldlandtrust.org

Energy/carbon saving
www.carbonrationing.org.uk
www.cat.org.uk
www.cdmgoldstandard.org
www.energysavingtrust.org.uk
www.lowcarbonbuildings.org.uk
www.nef.org.uk

Funerals
www.naturaldeath.org.uk

Gardening
www.flowers.org.uk
www.gardenorganic.org.uk
www.rhs.org.uk

Green power
www.ebico.co.uk
www.ecotricity.co.uk

Money
www.ethicalinvestment.org.uk

Recycling/swapping

www.freecycle.org
www.lets-linkup.com
www.recycle-more.co.uk
www.recycle.co.uk
www.recyclenow.com
www.swapxchange.org

Sustainable consumerism

www.fairtrade.org.uk
www.fsc.org
www.greenchoices.org
   (directory of green retailers)
www.soilassociation.org

Travel

www.aito.com.
www.green-business.co.uk
www.responsibletravel.com
www.thetravelfoundation.org.uk

Water

www.environment-agency.gov.uk

brilliant ideas

This book is published by Infinite Ideas, creators of the acclaimed **52 Brilliant Ideas** series. If you found this book helpful, here are some other titles in the **Brilliant Little Ideas** series which you may also find interesting.

- **Be incredibly healthy:** 52 brilliant little ideas to look and feel fantastic
- **Create your dream house and garden:** 52 brilliant little ideas for big home improvements
- **Enjoy great sleep:** 52 brilliant little ideas for bedtime bliss
- **Find your dream job:** 52 brilliant little ideas for total career success
- **Get fit:** 52 brilliant little ideas to win at the gym
- **Love your bump:** 52 brilliant little ideas for a happy pregnancy
- **Quit smoking for good:** 52 brilliant little ideas to kick the habit
- **Relax:** 52 brilliant little ideas to chill out
- **Seduce anyone:** 52 brilliant little ideas for being incredibly sexy
- **Shape up your life:** 52 brilliant little ideas for becoming the person you want to be
- **The laid-back wine guide:** 52 brilliant little ideas for free-thinking drinking
- **Win at winter sports:** 52 brilliant little ideas for skiing and snowboarding

For more detailed information on these books and others published by Infinite Ideas please visit www.infideas.com.

See reverse for order form.

Qty	Title	RRP
	Be incredibly creative	£4.99
	Create your dream house & garden	£4.99
	Enjoy great sleep	£5.99
	Find your dream job	£5.99
	Get fit	£5.99
	Love your bump	£4.99
	Quit smoking for good	£4.99
	Relax	£5.99
	Seduce anyone	£5.99
	Shape up your life	£5.99
	The laid-back wine guide	£4.99
	Win at winter sports	£4.99
	Add £2.49 postage per delivery address	
	TOTAL	

Name: ....

Delivery address: ....

....

....

E-mail:............................Tel (in case of problems): ....

By post Fill in all relevant details, cut out or copy this page and send along with a cheque made payable to Infinite Ideas. Send to: *Brilliant Little Ideas*, Infinite Ideas, 36 St Giles, Oxford OX1 3LD. **Credit card orders over the telephone** Call +44 (0) 1865 514 888. Lines are open 9am to 5pm Monday to Friday.

Please note that no payment will be processed until your order has been dispatched. Goods are dispatched through Royal Mail within 14 working days, when in stock. We never forward personal details on to third parties or bombard you with junk mail. The prices quoted are for UK and RoI residents only. If you are outside these areas please contact us for postage and packing rates. Any questions or comments please contact us on 01865 514 888 or email info@infideas.com.